ANTARCTIC

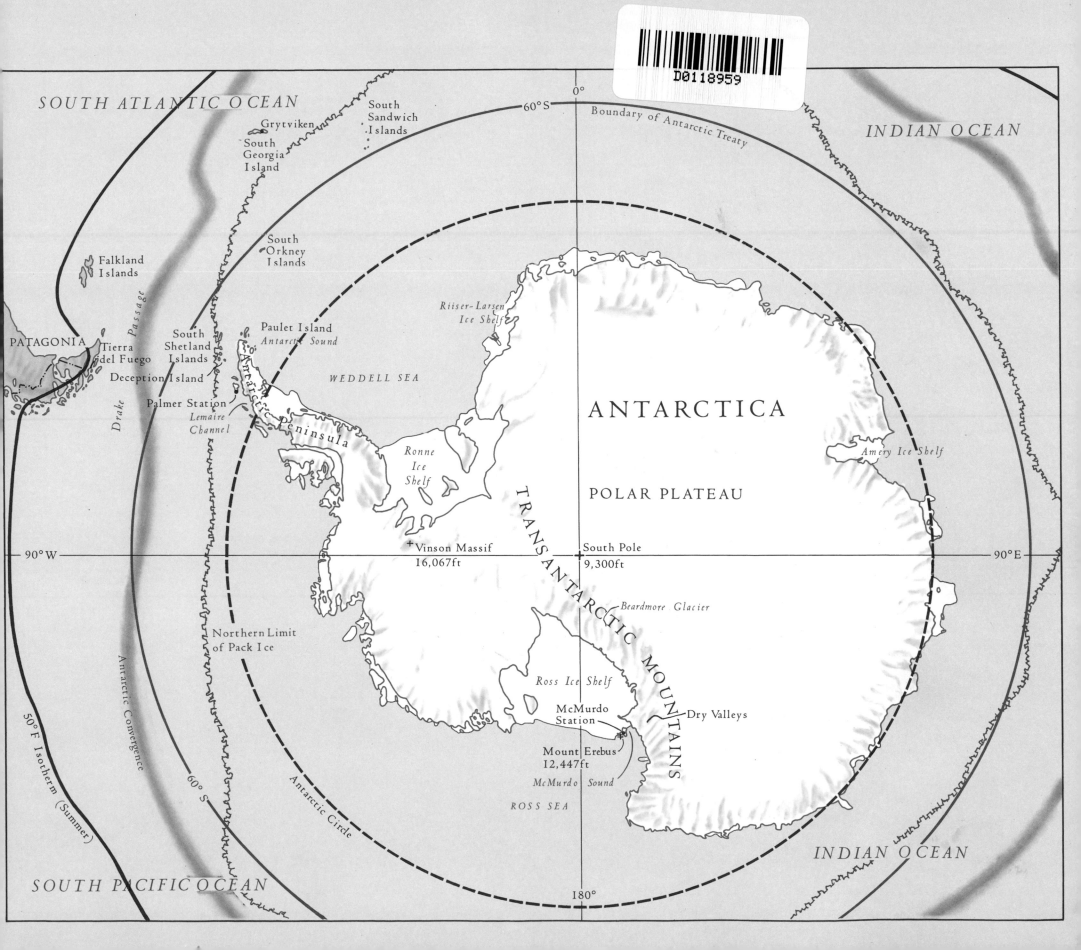

SOUTH ATLANTIC OCEAN

INDIAN OCEAN

South Sandwich Islands

Grytviken

South Georgia Island

Boundary of Antarctic Treaty

60°S

0°

South Orkney Islands

Falkland Islands

Riiser-Larsen Ice Shelf

Paulet Island

South Shetland Islands

Antarctic Sound

WEDDELL SEA

PATAGONIA

Tierra del Fuego

Deception Island

Palmer Station

Lemaire Channel

Antarctic Peninsula

Ronne Ice Shelf

Amery Ice Shelf

ANTARCTICA

POLAR PLATEAU

90°W

Vinson Massif 16,067ft

South Pole 9,300ft

90°E

TRANSANTARCTIC MOUNTAINS

Beardmore Glacier

Northern Limit of Pack Ice

Ross Ice Shelf

Dry Valleys

McMurdo Station

Mount Erebus 12,447ft

McMurdo Sound

ROSS SEA

50°F Isotherm (Summer)

Antarctic Convergence

60°S

Antarctic Circle

INDIAN OCEAN

SOUTH PACIFIC OCEAN

180°

Drake Passage

Poles Apart

POLES

PARALLEL VISIONS OF THE

A MOUNTAIN LIGHT PRESS BOOK PUBLISHED BY

A P A R T

ARCTIC AND ANTARCTIC

Text and photographs by *Galen Rowell*

MITCHELL BEAZLEY

First published in Great Britain in 1995 by Mitchell Beazley an imprint
of Reed Books, Michelin House, 81 Fulham Road, London SW3 6RB
and Auckland, Melbourne, Singapore and Toronto.

©1995 by Mountain Light Press

Additional photographs, pages 39, 111, 121, and 126,
by Barbara Cushman Rowell; page 91 by Bill Mackey;
page 125 by Jules Uberuaga

Endpaper maps created by Natural Science Illustrations
©1995, Robert W. Tope

Quotations from *Arctic Dreams* ©1986, Barry Lopez,
reprinted by permission

ISBN 1-857-32755-1

Printed in Hong Kong
9 8 7 6 5 4 3 2 1

Contents

Part One: Looking North, Looking South

67° North

54° South

The Arctic and the Antarctic are our last, vast wildernesses. Few people know them well.
On fine summer mornings as dawn mist floats over a river in the Brooks Range of Alaska
or as king penguins by the hundreds of thousands crowd a subantarctic stream on South
Georgia Island, the Far North and the Far South may appear deceptively temperate.

9

71° North

78° South

Stories of polar adventures make North and South seem alike: icy, empty, and cold. Here, a dog team in winter traverses the frozen Arctic Ocean off Barrow, Alaska, and a climber atop Mount Erebus looks out over the frozen Ross Sea of Antarctica.

74° North

78° South

Though they look much the same in photographs, these two landscapes are as different as Kansas and Kenya. Both show alpenglow on distant peaks over blue-shadowed pressure ridges of sea ice, yet the Arctic of northeast Greenland and the Antarctic of McMurdo Sound are biologically poles apart.

13

68° North

56° South

The Far North is America's Serengeti, while the Far South has no warm-blooded land animals on a continent that drifted into polar cold and isolation well before the age of mammals. Every warm-blooded Antarctic creature is bound to the sea. The Circumpolar North has a sense of the familiar, with bear, deer, buttercups, and Inuit all around the Arctic in North America, Asia, and Greenland. The South, having evolved in isolation from the world we know, feels distinctly more exotic and unfamiliar. In the North, caribou run through the lush summer meadows of the Brooks Range, while in the South, chinstrap penguins cling to an iceberg near the world's largest rookery, on Zavadovsky Island, where about 12 million penguins breed.

58° North

71° South

The polar bear—or ice bear, as it is called in many European languages—is found only in the
Arctic, the realm of the bear. The word *arctic* comes from the Greek *arktos*, meaning bear.
The Antarctic—or *anti-arktos*—is a realm without bears, where flightless penguins can live
and breed on the ice with no fear of land predators. Antarctica would be polar bear heaven
for about ten years.

17

71° North

72° South

The Arctic has had human residents for tens of thousands of years, while in the Antarctic, every human being is a visitor. The Circumpolar North consists of lands directly connected to those in which most of the world's population lives. Inuit cultures are spread around the globe in Arctic Canada, Greenland, Siberia, and Alaska, where these Inupiat Eskimos walk beside the frozen Arctic Ocean in winter. At a remote and recently discovered emperor penguin rookery, one of the first tourists decided to dress for the occasion.

19

What shocked me most about the polar regions on my first travels was neither the cold nor the remoteness, but a bewildering confrontation with my own lack of understanding. Looking at picture books and reading epic tales of exploration hadn't adequately prepared me for the loss of basic rhythms—as universal as the sunrise—that my body and mind have always taken for granted. In the seventies, during my first midsummer week on the Arctic Slope of the Brooks Range, time flowed without punctuation as days merged into undark nights and mornings arrived with no sunrise. Not only was my sense of time confused, but also my sense of place was weakened by the distinct feeling that I had entered a world without borders.

Traveling to the extreme polar latitudes creates a far more powerful disorientation than the jet lag that disrupts the biological clock of those who travel rapidly to distant longitudes. During those first days in the Arctic I felt as if I were on a different planet, with a different sun that did bizarre things in the sky.

The polar regions defy simple definition. They do not follow the Arctic and Antarctic Circles any more than America's highway system follows grid lines of latitude and longitude. The very qualities that set them "poles apart" from the rest of the world fail to translate into the sort of singularly distinct boundaries that define oceans or nations. Political borders often follow geographical features, such as rivers, coastlines, or mountain ranges, but none trace any part of the polar circles. Standing on the edge of the Arctic Circle is such a nonevent that even the most discerning eye detects no difference in the landscape or the life upon it from the south side to the north.

Demarking the boundaries of the polar regions is a far more complex task than drawing perfect circles at 66° 33' to match the earth's tilt where the sun never sets for at least one day each year. Like fairy-tale realms, the true polar regions seamlessly merge with each person's known world until their mysteries begin to stand out in bold relief. And since polar experts don't share the same known worlds, they have different answers to such basic questions as "What does Arctic mean?"

Only some geographers and cartographers point to the circles on their maps with certitude and answer, "the region beyond the Arctic Circle." Botanists just as assuredly respond, "life zones beyond treeline," adding that regions above the highest trees at more southerly latitudes fit within the same Arctic zone as those north of the trees. Marine biologists say, "the southern limit of the winter pack ice," with a few extra twists that follow the juncture of water masses. Climatologists and land biologists strongly suggest "areas north of the 50°F summer isotherm," an invisible boundary of average temperature that, compared with the Arctic Circle, has a sharply defined effect upon plant and animal life. Earth scientists prefer "the southern limit of the continuous permafrost" with the same conviction that social scientists generally include "all of Finland, Sweden, Norway, Iceland, Greenland, Labrador, northern Quebec, the Northwest Territories, the Yukon, Alaska above the Panhandle, and the Russian North."

Attempts to briefly define the polar regions always end up as mushy as the tundra in the spring, or wildly inaccurate. Each definition above is valid as far as it goes, and media reports are often as geographically skewed as the famous sketch of a New Yorker's map of North America.

20

Even though I give the press clear information about each upcoming lecture in which I will compare the Arctic and the Antarctic, inevitably at least one news story reports that I will be talking about the North and South Poles. Although I've been to both poles, neither my lecture nor this book is about the poles any more than a book on North America is about Manhattan.

To confront polar misconceptions head-on, I decided that this book would open with a series of bold Arctic/Antarctic comparisons. Inspiring readers to care about places they do not know and cannot easily define is indeed a major challenge. The Arctic and the Antarctic gained a strong identity for me only after I began to learn how they differ from each other and from the rest of the world. I came to realize that these vital parts of our planet that make up roughly 15 percent of the earth's land area are the last, vast regions so little changed by human activity. If enough people gain this perspective, the polar regions are destined to become the twenty-first century's metaphor for wildness.

As last frontiers, the polar regions are still perceived as wastelands; we should keep in mind, however, that many of the nineteenth century's "useless wastelands"—Death Valley, Mono Lake, Monument Valley—have undergone a complete reversal in public perception and are now considered places of wild beauty to be set aside for posterity.

Human existence depends upon the evolutionary flow of life that our ancestors took for granted in the temperate latitudes; that flow of life now continues least interrupted in the seemingly hostile polar regions. A positive role reversal for places historically regarded as inhospitable wasteland is happening by default. The polar regions remain much the same, while most of the change is happening in the rest of the world.

We tend to see the polar regions, like the faces of a foreign race, as having a similar look. Without clear comparisons, their differences are likely to escape us. For example, the North Pole sits in the middle of an ocean surrounded by land, while the South Pole is at 9,300 feet in the middle of a continent surrounded by ocean. Antarctica is not only the coldest, but also the driest, highest, and windiest of all the continents.

Everyone knows that polar bears live in the ice and snow. But where? Pictures from Alaska and Greenland fail to communicate whether or not they are also found in Antarctica. A practical joke played on military personnel shortly after their arrival at the main United States research station in Antarctica takes advantage of this confusion. Many navy personnel are visibly taken aback by a large poster they see on the wall when they report to the field center, unarmed, for overnight survival training out on the ice. Although elsewhere in the station posters of Fiji or Paris serve as pleasant wall decorations, the sight of the Canadian poster warning of polar bear attacks triggers a terrifying false assumption.

Modern maps of polar explorations bear a disturbing resemblance to historical maps of the American West. Paths of explorers cross broad white areas presumed to be wholly wild. Trade routes connect sparse settlements, mainly on the coasts. In the same way as a line on a map drawn long ago to mark the transcontinental railroad anticipated the rapid demise of the wild herds of the Great Plains, the Trans-Alaska Pipeline across the Brooks Range has already transcended its original purpose: the gravel road beside the seemingly ever more benign pipe has become a human conduit into the Arctic for private enterprise and pioneers in Ford Explorers.

The two national parks that were supreme metaphors of wildness during my youth, Yosemite and Yellowstone, have noticeably lost their luster. Despite the fact that their backcountry appears as wild and roadless as ever, these flagships of the national park system have become sullied. The romance these sacred natural shrines held during the era of my mother's first visit in 1916 and well into that of my own in 1943 is clearly over. Their beauty remains little changed, yet we now view it with the more critical eye of a spurned lover. The naive idea that political and geographical separation alone would save wild places began to vanish at about the time two closely spaced world wars erased the all-too-similar American conceit that had led us into isolationist policies intended to keep us forever out of war and apart from daily world affairs.

We have now come to the sad realization that the ecosystems of our parks in the lower forty-eight may well not survive as small islands of wildness that represent America as it once was. The increasing pressures of the modern world are cutting off much of the old evolutionary flow. It may be more than coincidence that the rangers mandated to defend these final enclaves continue to wear anachronistic flat hats and uniforms much like those worn by the troops we were about to send "over there" in the war that was supposed to end all wars at the time the National Park Service was created, in 1916.

To introduce the Arctic and the Antarctic, I have chosen to make liberal use of analogy and metaphor. The personal cognitive maps we use to navigate our way through life are sketched by past experience held in memory. Just as no map has meaning without symbolism we recognize or can look up on a chart, comprehension of environments quite unlike our own escapes us unless we can relate them to the world we know.

The first step toward understanding the polar regions is to develop a sense of place about the Arctic and the Antarctic that makes them as separate in our minds as Austria and Australia, New York and San Francisco, or the Himalaya and the Adirondacks. Direct photographic comparisons make the similarities and differences come alive in ways not always apparent even to those who have actually visited both polar realms.

90° North

The North Pole is at sea level in the middle of an ocean surrounded by land, while the South Pole is at 9,300 feet in the middle of the earth's highest continent, surrounded by oceans that isolate it from all other lands. Permanent fixtures cannot be built at the North Pole because it is located on pack ice that constantly drifts at least 1 mile per hour. Atop glacial ice 840 miles inland from the nearest navigable seas, the metal dome of the United States Amundsen-Scott South Pole Station also drifts, but only about 30 feet per year. If the Antarctic ice sheet were to melt, the continent would no longer be the earth's highest in terms of mean elevation.

Only when we know something of these places can we begin to appreciate their interconnectedness with each other and the rest of the world. Understanding and appreciation grow out of active mental involvement and questioning rather than passive ingestion of facts. My hope is that with understanding, the reader will feel a sense of responsibility for the future condition of these most pristine areas of the earth at the very time when they have become most vulnerable to change from without.

The three sections of this book have been structured to give the reader a great degree of choice about how to enjoy it—as a page-turner with lively captions or as an interactive personal exploration. When an image in Part One or Two raises questions unanswered by the immediate caption, the reader can refer to essays in Part Three that describe each situation in greater detail, as well as how it was photographed. Both thumbnail images and page numbers key the essays to the photographs.

In the parallel visions of Part One, the Arctic image is always on the left-hand page, the Antarctic on the right, accompanied by a notation of the degrees of latitude north or south to further key a clear sense of place. Captions focus more on the overall impression created by the pairings than on the specific content of individual images, which is developed in more detail in the essays in Part Three.

Part Two continues the theme of parallel visions at a slower pace with twenty-four short picture stories. Comparison of single photographs gives way to two-page spreads of three to six photographs each, focused on a polar theme, alternating between North and South. Additionally, every photograph in Part Two is described in a separate essay in Part Three.

Readers who do not already possess a clear idea of polar boundaries will want to study carefully the pairs of maps on the endpapers before moving beyond the first few pairs of images. By referring to the maps while reading the next few paragraphs of this introduction, readers will understand that the polar regions extend beyond the polar circles for far more compelling reasons than the concerns of scientists already mentioned.

World maps breed serious misunderstanding when they indicate polar areas only by the arbitrary circles where the tilt of the earth's axis creates at least one day when the sun does not set in summer and one day when the sun does not rise in winter. I have come to believe that these precise polar circles, because of the confusion they create, should be left off maps designed to show only clear political boundaries, natural features, and human settlements. By emphasis, those circles distort reality in much the same way that the placement on a road map of a single mountain that is not a region's highest or most important sets up a fragment of truth likely to misrepresent information of potentially greater importance. For example, pilots dare not trust the limited truths

on such maps. If they did, conceivably they could fly over the highest marked elevations only to crash into an even higher, unmarked mountain. Similarly, travelers often know in their bones that they are in the Arctic, or the Antarctic, when in fact they are not within those circles on the map.

If we were to strictly follow the circles as Arctic and Antarctic boundaries, we would be forced to conclude that most of the 8,500 people who paid dearly to go on Antarctic cruises last year in fact never saw the Antarctic. The peninsula visited by the great majority of tourists juts well to the north of the circle into an area where marine wildlife is most abundant. It is indeed part of the Antarctic continent and clearly inside other Antarctic boundaries that geographers and biologists have demarked. Similarly, many other distinctly Antarctic or Arctic regions lie outside the simplistic circles.

Another factor to consider is that the polar circles are not the constants we imagine them to be. They move about 200 miles every 40,000 years in what are called Milankovitch Cycles. These changes in the earth's tilt parallel many, but not all, ice age events. The first humans to visit northern Iceland stood within the true Arctic Circle, where the sun does not set at least one day a year, but today's visitors do not, unless they visit a remote island off the coast.

In Alaska's Denali National Park, which lies about 200 miles south of the Arctic Circle, there are days when the sun never sets on the 20,320-foot summit of Mount McKinley. The peak's extreme height catches low-angled rays aimed toward the circle, and the climate around its summit is Arctic in the extreme. Even near its base, at an elevation of just 2,800 feet, the expanse of open tundra above treeline fits Arctic definitions of climate and vegetation.

The endpaper maps created especially for this book include a number of lines that define polar climates far better than the polar circles do. Land biologists prefer to use the more wiggly line of the 50°F summer isotherm—the average air temperature of the warmest month. This temperature boundary roughly, but not exactly, follows treeline in the Far North. It skirts inside the Arctic Circle across Europe and Alaska, yet dips much farther south across Greenland and eastern Canada, helping explain why polar bears are found around Churchill, Manitoba.

In the Antarctic region of the Far South, however, where marine life is dominant and there are no trees on the continent or islands immediately surrounding it, biologists prefer to use the ever-shifting edge of the Antarctic Convergence, a sharply defined ocean boundary where cold waters driven by winds off the Antarctic continent abruptly merge with more temperate waters. That line is more fuzzy than others on the map because the convergence moves in response to changes in currents and powerful katabatic winds caused by heavier cold air constantly flowing downward off the chilly heights of the southern continent over its coasts.

The huge Antarctic ice cap and its great winds push the 50°F summer isotherm a full 900 miles outside the Antarctic Circle over the tip of South America, at a latitude comparable to that of England in the north. Further complicating the issue, another circle on the map follows an arbitrary political line drawn at latitude 60° south by the Antarctic Treaty of 1959, which established a global commons limiting military activity and environmental impact.

In summary, we most commonly judge what is Arctic by land climate and what is Antarctic by sea climate. For most purposes the 50°F summer isotherm of the Arctic and the Antarctic Convergence come closest to singularly demarking these vast regions.

In 1993, the year after I had traveled to the South Pole and around the Antarctic continent as a participant in the National Science Foundation (NSF) Antarctic Artists and Writers program, my wife, Barbara, and I attended the first-ever conference of past grant recipients. Surprisingly, nineteen of the twenty-five grantees since 1958 showed up. Those who didn't attend were either no longer alive, overseas, or still working "on the ice." We had been invited to present "perspectives that can enrich future human involvement with Antarctica," yet we were not to address the subject as if we were responding to an NSF request. Shared ideas were posted on the walls and organized under broad headings such as environmental protection, the roles of the NSF and the U.S. government, and the relationship between art and science. By far the largest category was "Our roles and responsibilities as artists/writers."

My previous experience with group discussions concerning the inner motives of successful photographers or writers had led me to expect a regurgitation of First Amendment rights, that is, that we can express ourselves any way we please. In fact, that right of art and the media has never reigned supreme. We pursue our crafts in the shadow of an economic imperative that compels us to consent to the whims of the editors, curators, and ad agencies who butter our bread and pick up our expenses. Their covert selection processes, hidden from the public eye, censor free expression as effectively as dictatorships. Those who complain too much simply disappear from the loop.

Early on, the great nature writer Barry Lopez shared his feelings with us about the current American obsession with self. "We are living in a time of desperate spiritual hunger," he mused, describing how Americans have come to devote their energies to issues of personal autonomy instead of social responsibility, both as individuals and as a nation.

Our group strongly agreed that the rare Antarctic experience afforded us by the NSF with no control over our output should not be used to foster art forms that emphasize obsessions of self over honest interpretations of place. I was surprised to hear an informal debate about the Antarctic photography of a deceased NSF grantee, Eliot Porter, who in the seventies had produced a major book that portrayed the continent without human presence—although even then, the U.S. research station at McMurdo had the crude sprawl of a frontier bush town.

One of the writers suggested that because the book implied a documentation of Antarctica, a Porter photograph or two of the aesthetically shocking base might have averted the continued pollution that came to a head with media confrontations between the NSF and Greenpeace, international loss of face, and a $37-million cleanup (that the NSF insists was already in the works). Even the prestigious journal *Science* reported how McMurdo had "pumped raw sewage into the Ross Sea, burned its garbage in the open air, bulldozed debris into Winter Quarters Bay, or piled it on the ice, waiting for the spring thaw to carry it out to sea."

The NSF has managed all U.S. research stations in Antarctica since 1971. Projects are planned long in advance, limited resources are very expensive, and uninvited guests are unwelcome. Beyond the peninsula where the cruise ships sail, access to the main continent of Antarctica depends upon NSF support, a military posting, support from another nation's science base, or an extremely expensive private expedition. Thus the NSF Artists and Writers Program, combined with the reports of a handful of invited news journalists, has, to a great degree, shaped the public's vision and provided the only counterbalance to scientific and governmental publications that tend to favor facts without emotional interpretation.

Our group agreed that the privileged access we each had applied for and been granted created a special responsibility to produce art that communicated the truths we had realized. Our philosophy was similar to that voiced by the astronaut Rusty Schweickart after his visit to an even more remote environment: "It comes through to you so powerfully that you're the sensing element for humanity."

A few months after the NSF meeting, Barbara and I traveled to the North Pole as photography lecturers aboard a Russian nuclear icebreaker with a crew of 156. The ship had been chartered by Quark Expeditions to take us from the eastern tip of Siberia through the frozen Arctic Ocean across the entire Northeast Passage. After visiting the pole, we ended the journey at Murmansk, the world's largest town north of the Arctic Circle, with a population of over half a million.

Our "expedition cruise" was the most incongruous journey of my life. As multicourse meals were served on white linen, house-size blocks of ice split off the bow with the sound of thunder and the shaking of a 9.0 earthquake. Some couples rarely looked outside and passed the time playing bridge, while a Swiss woman in her mid-eighties became an

62° North

65° South

A lush meadow at latitude 62° north in the Cirque of the Unclimbables of Canada's Northwest Territories is at a comparable latitude to that at which vast glaciers plunge into the Antarctic seas of the Lemaire Channel in the South. The huge Antarctic ice sheet supercools the South to a climatic equivalent of at least 10 degrees higher latitude in the North. This explains why 50° south feels at least as frigid as 60° north and why a cruise through the mountains of the Antarctic Peninsula has a mythical feeling, as if one were floating through the Himalaya.

almost permanent fixture out on the top deck, where she stood for hours bundled up in a huge parka watching the ship cut through 6 feet of pack ice at 14 knots.

Over tea one afternoon somewhere north of 85°, a woman from Indiana told us that whenever she had mentioned heading for the North Pole on her vacation, friends gave her a blank stare. They were embarrassed to display their ignorance by asking if the North Pole is on land or sea, for example, or if polar bears eat penguins, or if polar vacations have become a fad.

When Barbara and I repeated this story on our return, few of our friends laughed. They were more likely to ask, "You mean there aren't penguins in the North?" "There are polar bears in the South, aren't there?" "Will you sail to the South Pole, too?"

These experiences emphasized the pitfalls of trying to present the Arctic and the Antarctic in photographs to those who have never been there. Polar landscapes are especially devoid of subject matter that we clearly recognize. When we do see something familiar, we unconsciously infer that the picture is about that—a penguin or a polar bear, for example —and nothing more. We tend to ignore parts of a picture that we can't compare to our known world.

A conscious goal of my polar photography has been to create images that move beyond the limitations of instant comprehension toward a greater relevance. I decided to try direct North/South comparisons early on, but received lukewarm feedback from friends to sketchy slide shows of my work-in-progress. I continued imagining direct comparisons of images, both while working in the field and after the fact. Reading about polar phenomena helped me visualize new pairings of the 40,000 images I had taken. I would wake up in the night and scrawl a note about putting a breaching whale beside a penguin erupting from the sea, for example.

All perception operates by comparison. No photograph moves us unless it triggers the memory of a pattern or form that we have seen before. If an image is made up entirely of original, unfamiliar subject matter, we simply cannot comprehend it and so pass it by. On the other hand, if an image is so entirely comprehensible at first glance that it lacks all sense of mystery, we often find it boring. The power of photography to captivate our senses, to teach us something new, to hold a sense of mystery that intrigues us, is contained in the way its balance of the familiar and unfamiliar forces us to extrapolate beyond what we already know.

When I first cruised the Antarctic Peninsula, I had the chance to adjust gradually to the sights of the first icebergs and ice-capped islands, but when I flew with the NSF in a military C141 to the Antarctic continent later that year, I felt a strong sense of perceptual disorientation the moment I stepped off the plane. Virtually all first-timers feel it and chalk it up to the mystery of the place. Even after my previous Antarctic trip, the landscape in the deep South seemed profoundly different from the image that movies and still photographs had created in my mind. Here was a warning that my work, too, would be deficient in the kind of familiar symbolism that allows us to clearly recognize a face, a sign, or a tree.

For me, the Arctic and the Antarctic have become metaphors, not only for wildness itself, but also for the myriad significant things about the earth's wild places that cannot be expressed in words or images. In a modern world bent upon becoming a theme park of artificial visual inputs it is important to realize that photographs never catch it all.

Despite reading about the polar regions in school, few of us hold anything close to an accurate perception of what they are, how they compare, and the countless ways in which they affect the parts of the world we inhabit. My own failure to become enchanted with the polar regions until middle age is directly related to the failure of most polar photographs to hold my attention. Images of explorers holding up flags at points said to be the poles lack the visual context of a 1953 news photograph that captivated me when I was twelve. It showed Tenzing Norgay standing on the summit of Mount Everest for the first time. The steep-angled snow beneath Tenzing's feet ended abruptly, with no more upness. The image evoked a strong sense of place—atop a singular and cold natural feature. Two years earlier I had stood on such a snowy spot on top of a mere 10,000-foot mountain in the High Sierra of my home state of California. Below me was not an endless expanse of snow and ice, as in polar photographs, but a hauntingly familiar landscape of lakes, forests, and a distant meadow where I was camped for two weeks with my parents on a Sierra Club annual outing.

Each summer I hiked back into the High Sierra with my family, into a world ever more simplified by increments of altitude. I loved the sight of clean alpine meadows, well above timberline, dotted with flowers and boulders, but I failed to make the connection that, regardless of the California summer beneath my feet, I was indeed standing in the Arctic life zone of my planet in these meadows and on the summits of Sierra peaks.

It was no coincidence that the byword of early Sierra Club outings was "Life begins at ten thousand feet," because that altitude in California coincides with a well-defined polar boundary. The life zone at 10,000 feet in the Sierra just below timberline is called "Hudsonian" by biologists because its climate and vegetation closely match those of the region beside Hudson Bay near the northern treeline. The next higher life zone, where I stood upon that snowy summit in summer, is called "Arctic/Alpine" because a similar climate is found both at high latitudes in the Arctic and at high altitudes in the Alps.

Even after several summers of hikes into the snowy Sierra, books of polar exploration continued to leave me cold, so to speak. My eyes would search in vain across great white landscapes printed on white pages for a hint of the familiar to render an impression of something more than a great white blank. I was left, however, with the distinct feeling that the polar regions were as irrelevant as they were bleak. Besides, why should I be concerned with polar explorers who always seemed to be struggling, suffering, dying, negating each other's claims, and publishing photographs that gave me little sense of place? Climbers seemed not only to be having more fun, but also to be reaching summits that fascinated me both in person and in photographs. Books on mountains whetted my young appetite and set me on the path of climbing, exploring, understanding, and interpreting mountains of the world.

I feel compelled to relate the strong polar disinterest of my youth because of a recurring thought that has come to me in such places as the bottom of a steaming ice cave atop an Antarctic volcano and out on the Arctic Ocean whaling with Eskimos. What would happen if I failed to return? I imagine someone looking through my library and personal files for the earliest record of the polar passion that led inexorably toward my end. They would believe they had found it in a rare first edition of a nineteenth-century book on Arctic exploration graced with a 1952 inscription: "For Galen on his graduation from Hillside School as an Arctic explorer." I was eleven years old at the time.

Further searching might reveal an enigma. Only a smattering of other polar books found a way into my library until almost four decades later, when I undertook most of my twenty-odd journeys into high latitudes. Like a rare, unexplained fossil, the old book sits apart from the known record, begging answers to questions not asked before its discovery. It was written by a man who later died searching for Sir John Franklin, who had died searching for the Northwest Passage.

A decade ago I would have shrugged off the inscribed book as an anomaly in my life. I lay no claim whatsoever to a lifelong fascination with the Arctic and the Antarctic, and yet in a larger sense the old book has much to do with the shaping of this one. Its text is so convoluted that, searching for clarification, I turned to my father's encyclopedia, where short entries about the explorer helped me make sense of what he had so incompletely communicated in his book. I remember vowing then that I would never write a book like that, knowing with the certitude of youth that active involvement with books was somewhere in my destiny but that polar exploration was not.

The story of how I acquired the old book begins with my father, a professor of philosophy, reading me jungle, mountain, and polar adventure stories from the time I was three. Before my seventh Christmas, he admonished family and friends not to give me children's books, suggesting far too prematurely that my reading comprehension was approaching his own. The heavy packages under the tree that year contained no toys. Among the new additions to my library was an advanced reference book on medieval mythology that I couldn't fathom. The weighty Arctic exploration book my neighbors gave me four years later may have been chosen at least as much for its incomprehensibility as for its subject.

Though I could read most of the words in the big adult books I was given, I was often unable to assemble them into patterns that held a larger meaning for me because their context was entirely too foreign. I now recognize that inability to comprehend as similar to our perception of a polar photograph as empty or, at best, mysterious—we are unable to mentally reassemble unfamiliar visual symbols into something that is either close to the original scene or meaningful.

As I have mentioned, part of our failure to decode polar imagery comes from our lack of direct experience with the landscape, but an even larger part is that we lack development of the proper "hardware" in our eyes and "software" in our brains to interpret typical polar realities. Our visual system evolved in more temperate latitudes in response to a broader and somewhat different assortment of cues. Everyday life simply doesn't prepare us to see polar photographs, especially when so many relevant visual constructs of size, color, and form are missing that we would create a somewhat twisted and inaccurate rendition of the real scene if it were before our eyes. Gone, for example, is the atmospheric perspective that normally evokes distance. As an Antarctic scientist from Los Angeles quipped, "I don't trust air I can't reach out and touch." It is little wonder that we so often fail to respond emotionally to polar scenes in the secondary medium of photographs.

In the 1990s, when I began visiting the polar regions with thoughts of producing a book, I was both captivated by what I saw and worried—my early lack of interest had stemmed from the same secondary visual input of photographs such as the ones I was about to create. Thus many of my favorite images didn't make the final cut. Though they evoke a strong response to the beauty of the natural landscape, they communicate a lesser sense of place and interconnectedness than some of the images finally chosen, which simply would not stand on their own as exhibit photographs.

Had I produced this book as simply a collection of my finest polar photographs, it might have been little more than a slick version of that first polar book of my youth. Readers would have needed to look elsewhere to figure out what was before their eyes on these pages. The message of the enduring nature and importance of the last, vast wild places on Earth would not have been revealed between these covers.

71° North

67° South

Polar cold blurs the clear distinction between land and sea that we take for granted along the coastlines of the rest of the world. Winter ice on the Arctic Ocean merges with frozen tundra near Barrow, Alaska, but what you're seeing in the Weddell Sea of Antarctica is not a coast at all. Open ocean merges into seasonal ice that locks an iceberg temporarily in place, while what appears to be land far in the distance is in fact a vast floating ice shelf 100 miles off the continent's shore.

Trees often grow north of the Arctic Circle, but Antarctica has none at all. Boreal forest covers parts of the Brooks Range of Alaska as well as parts of Arctic Siberia and Scandinavia. The Dry Valleys of Antarctica are the most lifeless areas on Earth; the empty landscape is broken only by the strange shapes of ventifacts—barren rocks carved by millions of years of wind.

67° North

33

77° South

62° North

62° South

The Antarctic continent has only these two species of flowering plants and almost no fly-ing insects, while Arctic tundra has hundreds of kinds of flowers and thousands of insects, including many that disturb wildlife and humans. Antarctica's largest land animal is a tiny wingless fly. One benefit of a summer vacation in the Antarctic is that there are no bugs.

84° North

78° South

Antarctica has the richest summer seas in the world. Here, breaking sea ice north of Greenland lacks the verdant bloom of plankton that coats the underside of Antarctic sea ice in McMurdo Sound, 15 feet below the surface. The deeper, less windy seas of the cloudier Arctic receive less sunlight and oxygenation. Only a few select areas of the Far North are as rich in sea life as Antarctic waters.

These favorite icons of the polar regions reflect a human demeanor with their upright stance, but they depart from the typical behavior of their animal families in more significant ways. This adolescent king penguin must molt into adult plumage as a flightless bird before it can survive the change of realms into the seas that all warm-blooded creatures of the Far South depend upon for sustenance. A move from land into water accounts for the greater size of the subarctic Alaskan brown bear, compared with the rest of the grizzly family. During the annual salmon run, its protein uptake radically increases, and dominance battles over prime fishing spots favor larger bears.

59° North

54° South

25° North

Neither of these creatures breaching out of the sea is a fish. The enormous Arctic gray whale evolved from a much smaller walking mammal, while the emperor penguin evolved from a flying bird into a 60-to-90-pound living torpedo that erupts from the water onto a high ice edge with a belly full of food for its chick. The annual journey of the gray whale from its home in Arctic seas to breed in lagoons on the coast of Mexico is the longest migration of any mammal.

83° North

78° South

A polar bear diving into the Arctic Ocean at 83° north above Svalbard has evolved into a true marine mammal, capable of living entirely off the sea and swimming across 100 miles of open water. Descended from coastal brown bears that ventured into fresh water to fish for salmon and probably discovered seals where the rivers met the sea, the polar bear evolved white fur, broad feet, and powerful swimming ability to hunt for seals out on the floating sea ice. The mysterious mummy seals of the Dry Valleys of Antarctica were discovered naturally freeze-dried up to 50 miles inland and 2,000 feet above the sea. Though some look as if they died last week, some individuals have been determined—by carbon-14 dating—to be thousands of years old. Perhaps not all of these juvenile crabeater seals would have starved and frozen if Antarctica had stayed put 100 million years ago in the temperate latitudes. A reversal of their adaptation from land to sea might well have created Antarctica's first land mammal.

43

58° North

44

78° South

A polar bear mother guards her cubs from marauding males on the edge of Hudson Bay in a blizzard, while a Weddell seal mother in Antarctica, moments after birth, has no apparent fear. Her bewildered pup has just emerged from a tight, dark world 99°ғ above zero into a vast, bright one 20°ғ below zero.

65° North

54° South

The largest polar seals—the Pacific walrus of the Arctic and the southern elephant seal of the Antarctic—may weigh up to 3,500 pounds and 8,000 pounds, respectively. Whalers and sealers wiped out an estimated 85 percent of the walrus population in the brief period between 1869 and 1878. A single ship would take up to 700 in only a couple of days. By 1908, the strange, tusked creature, called a "whale-horse" by Scandinavian whalers, was thought to be nearly extinct. Official protection began with a hunting ban in U.S. waters. In the South, the vast elephant seal populations also have recovered from near extinction.

47

65° North

54° South

Reindeer graze the tundra of both the Far North and the Far South. The unlikely sight of reindeer wandering amidst penguins on the subantarctic island of South Georgia is a result of Scandinavian whalers importing reindeer to raise them for meat. When the island was abandoned in 1965, the reindeer took to the wilds. They appear healthy and robust until compared with their domestic Siberian cousins, which have been herded by Chukchi natives since prehistoric times.

Seabirds poles apart often coevolve similar adaptations of color and form. The horned puffin of the North and the macaroni penguin of the South share similar habitats on the shores of rugged islands above cold oceans. Despite obvious differences, their overall resemblance, including clownlike personae, comes across more clearly in direct photographic comparisons than in actual observations of each bird at opposite ends of the earth.

57° North

51

57° South

Thick-billed murres, heads pointed skyward, bear a surprising resemblance to Adélie penguins. The murres nest precariously on sea cliffs on the Pribilof Islands in the Bering Sea, beyond the reach of arctic foxes, while the penguins nest on flat ground at the edge of the Ross Ice Shelf at latitude 78° south, where there are no land predators.

53

78° South

80° North

61° South

Profiles of birds in flight at opposite ends of the earth may be more similar than the appearance of the birds at rest. The form of an immature ivory gull as it passes through a snowstorm on the coast of Franz Josef Land in the Russian Arctic anticipates the glide of a pintado petrel in a blizzard over the dark seas of the Antarctic Sound.

A raven's wing prints from a nearly failed takeoff on Alaska's Mount McKinley help explain why the wandering albatross could have evolved only in the southern oceans. Unbroken by land, the powerful circumpolar Antarctic winds of the legendary Roaring Forties and Furious Fifties enable the world's largest flying bird to remain in the air or float on the ocean for years without alighting on land. The raven, which had raided a climbers' camp at 16,000 feet, had a classic density-altitude problem trying to take off with a full load into thin, still air. The Arctic has no albatrosses.

63° North

54° South

58° North

The arctic fox that preys on northern seabird colonies turns white to match the winter terrain, but the most southern-dwelling fox, the Fuegian, does not. It lives on the edge of the Antarctic 50°F summer isotherm on the island of Tierra del Fuego, off the tip of South America. The Antarctic continent and the islands that immediately surround it have never had resident foxes.

63° South

These large predators of the Far North and Far South appear vastly different but share hidden similarities. Both the Alaskan brown bear and the Antarctic leopard seal often prey on fish and only occasionally attack humans. Although the leopard seal is best known for devouring unsuspecting penguins and seals, half of its diet consists of tiny, shrimplike krill. Half of the bear's diet is usually vegetarian. The skulls of some bears and seals are so similar that when they are removed from their habitats and placed unlabeled on a shelf, zoology students easily confuse them.

61

71° North

62

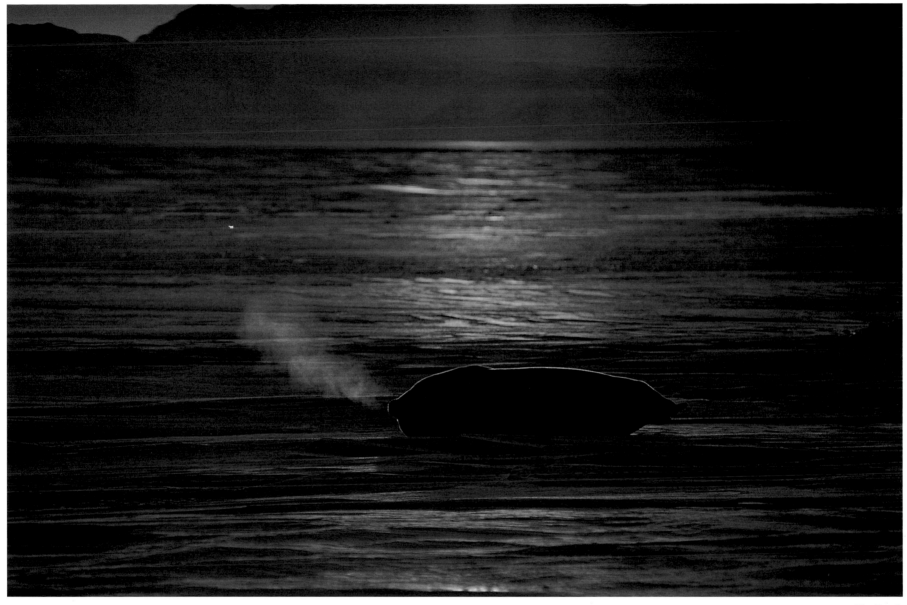

78° South

Human beings are at the top of the food chain of polar predators. While an Eskimo hunts wary bearded seals on the pack ice of the Arctic Ocean, a pregnant Weddell seal shows no fear of approach on the frozen Ross Sea beneath the Transantarctic Mountains, in a region protected by the Antarctic Treaty. Like other top predators, such as the peregrine falcon and the polar bear, native people who eat primarily seals or fish tend to bioaccumulate toxics to dangerous levels.

68° North

90° South

Arctic and Antarctic environmental protection are poles apart both geographically and politically. The destiny of Arctic wildlands is vested in independent decisions made by each Arctic nation. The United States alone decided whether to bisect the pristine Brooks Range with an oil pipeline. In contrast, these flags at the South Pole denote nations that signed the 1959 Antarctic Treaty, which created a veritable global commons for peaceful and scientific purposes. Forty-two nations have now acceded. The Protocol on Environmental Protection, signed in 1991, is as strict as the regulations in many national parks.

Eskimos normally travel armed to defend themselves against bears and to pursue subsistence hunting. Here, they are holding fat-barreled bomb guns designed to quickly dispatch harpooned whales as humanely as possible. Weapons are far less common in the South, because of the lack of land predators, except for humans. This pair of soldiers brandishing assault weapons in camouflage gear on the subantarctic island of South Georgia are Nepalese Gurkhas posted by the British after the 1982 Falklands war to discourage an Argentine invasion. The soldiers, Raj and Mahendra, come from villages beneath Mount Everest. Farther south, the Antarctic Treaty forbids armed manuevers.

54° South

Human predation has severely impacted marine mammal populations in both the North and the South. The tiny Pribilof Islands of Alaska once had the earth's largest single concentration of mammals and birds, but over 90 percent of the northern fur seals were gone by 1911. Under ever more strict control, the local Aleuts took up to 30,000 seals per year until the commercial hunt was discontinued in 1984. In the South, more than 1.3 million whales have been killed since 1920. Right, humpback, and blue whales of the subantarctic seas have been reduced to about 1 percent of historic numbers. The elderly son of a Falklands whaler made a late-life decision to switch sides and posted a notice of protest in his own backyard.

57° North

STOP KILLING
THE WHALES

52° South

71° North

While Eskimo subsistence whaling legally continues in the Arctic, a 1994 international treaty, which is openly flaunted by the Japanese and Russians, bans whaling south of latitude 40° in all the southern oceans except for a wedge down to 60° around South America. The action frozen by the camera—harpoon in midair between the arm of an Eskimo in a sealskin umiak and the back of an endangered bowhead whale—is part of what biologists call "the best-managed hunt on the planet" because of accurate population surveys, conservative quotas, and the absence of poaching. The growing popularity of Antarctic tourism emphasizes ever more clearly that killer whales frolicking beside a raft in Paradise Bay are most valuable alive.

71

A traditional Eskimo parka worn by an Inupiat Eskimo woman contrasts with the modern synthetics of an Antarctic guide. He could not afford her garment, nor would she want his. Her fine furs and handiwork would have to sell for thousands of dollars. She reserves this parka for special occasions and wears another traditional design for everyday use. Both were sewn by her mother, in patterns passed down from ancestors who invented the first parka long before polar explorers borrowed the concept.

73

78° South

71° North

78° South

The consistent Scandinavian architecture of Greenland pleases the eye; the conspicuously American jumble of cargo lines and squat metal buildings of "Mac Town" in Antarctica does not. Whereas the native residents of the Inuit village of Scoresbysund live there all year and have a stake in their town's destiny, the 1,600 scientists and support staff to McMurdo Station, the primary Antarctic research facility for the United States, are mainly summer visitors: few spend the winter, and fewer still have a role in future planning. A closer look belies the overall appearance of these two polar outposts, however. Beneath the snows of Scoresbysund is plenty of garbage, while McMurdo has had a major clean-up and boasts an active recycling program.

64° North

Polar climates have a remarkable capacity to hold items in suspended animation. From bow-head whale ribs left standing on the coast of Siberia by hunters more than 500 years ago, to the interior of Shackleton's 1907 Antarctic hut that looks as if he left it yesterday, time seems to stand still.

The flip side of the remarkable preservation of polar cultural artifacts is that scars on the landscape don't go away. The infamous "Hickel Highway" was used only in the winter of 1968 to haul oil exploration gear over the snows of the Brooks Range of Alaska without touching vegetation. The swath through Gates of the Arctic National Park remains highly visible a quarter century later. On Thule Island, just a half degree north of the 60° limit of the Antarctic Treaty, penguins nest in the toxic wreckage of an Argentine scientific base, destroyed by the British after the 1982 Falklands war and abandoned by both sides without a cleanup.

67° North

59° South

69° North

90° South

Polar progress requires tremendous amounts of imported energy. At Murmansk, the world's largest polar city, with a half-million inhabitants, a nuclear base for icebreakers and submarines remained top secret even after Mikhail Gorbachev announced his plan for an Arctic zone of peace in 1987. At the South Pole, a cache of aviation fuel left by a Saudi prince who sponsored a private American polar expedition is marked by a sign that gives the distances to Mecca in English and Arabic. Each 55-gallon drum is worth $7,500 in transportation costs alone.

81

82

The Arctic atmosphere is nowhere near as pristine as that of the unpopulated Far South. At a National Oceanic and Atmospheric Administration monitoring station on the Arctic coast of Alaska, a single week's worth of the circumpolar Arctic haze that drifts on prevailing winds from the industrialized world turns an air-sampling filter from white to black. A NASA experiment uses colder, cleaner Antarctica as a Mars analog to test robotic devices remotely controlled by a joy stick through a head-mounted display: an image moves to follow the operator's eye, thus creating a limited form of real-time virtual reality called telepresence, the sense of being somewhere else.

89° North

71° South

The Russian nuclear icebreaker *Yamal* cruises at 14 knots through 6 feet of pack ice en route to the North Pole, while the more conventional diesel icebreaker *Kapitan Khlebnikov* unloads a bevy of the first ship-based tourists onto an ice shelf in the Weddell Sea of Antarctica.

67° North

Among the visual rewards of polar adventures are the northern lights in winter, seen here above an Arctic camp in the Brooks Range, and giant towers of steaming ice backlit by the midnight sun near the summit crater of Mount Erebus, the world's southernmost known active volcano.

Part Two: Polar Short Stories

Mushing through the Brooks Range

Dogsledding—the classic means of Arctic transportation—has almost vanished as a traditional way of life. Eskimos, who long ago imported the idea from across the Bering Strait, gave up on it in the sixties in favor of snowmobiles that can be parked in the spring and not fed. In 1994, I joined a 100-mile winter expedition into Gates of the Arctic National Park organized by Sourdough Outfitters of Bettles. Six of us learned to run our own teams and headed out for a week. Our dogs were content to sleep in the open in subzero temperatures (*right*). Our guide, Bill Mackey, was an old hand who had raced the 1,100-mile Iditarod Trail. He used my camera to capture me as I crested a hill (*far right*); then I included my own shadow (*above*) in a more common perspective summed up by the one-liner "If you're not the lead dog, the view is always the same." What I will always remember is not the cold of the Arctic nights, but the glow (*right, above*) of the wood fire in the portable stove that warmed our insulated tent as the northern lights danced across the sky.

The Worst Journey in the World

Three members of Robert Scott's South Pole expedition left their Cape Evans hut to man-haul sledges 130 miles in -77°F temperatures during the long winter night of 1911. Their goal was to collect the elusive egg of an emperor penguin from a colony at Cape Crozier (*right, above*). Though they succeeded, the embryo did not show the flightless emperor to be the missing link between birds and dinosaurs, as they had hoped. Emperors evolved from flying birds breeding on a continent that drifted south into isolation and cold.

Eight decades later, I found the journey rugged even in spring daylight at -20°F or above. We used snowmobiles, except for the last miles, where a blizzard (*above*) repeatedly blew me off my feet. I had joined Dr. Gerald Kooyman (*left and right*) and his team of researchers in their quest for baseline data on this creature that breeds in one of the earth's most pristine places, to be used as a future biological monitor, "an early warning system of changes in the marine environment." The team visually surveyed the colony on the sea ice and attached telemetry to an emperor's back (*far right*) that has recorded dives into the sea as deep as 1,700 feet and as long as 17 minutes.

93

Science in the Arctic

Scientists in the Far North generally carry out their research with lower budgets and poorer facilities than those in the Far South. Although there are no towns in Antarctica to offer support for transportation and lodging, a presidential directive "to maintain an active and influential presence" on that continent benefits more than 2,500 U.S. scientists and support staff each year. Lewis Shapiro (*right*) of the University of Alaska cuts blocks of Arctic sea ice on a -32°F winter day to run structural tests on location. Jennelle Marcereau (*second right*) uses portable instrumentation inside a trailer at the Toolik Field Station on the north side of the Brooks Range in Alaska to test the buffering capacity of tundra groundwater to increasing levels of acid rain for the Marine Biological Laboratory of Woods Hole. A Canadian rocket launcher (*far right*) near Churchill, Manitoba, was built by the National Research Council to send test rockets over the North Pole to monitor electromagnetic phenomena in the upper atmosphere that create northern lights.

95

Science in the Antarctic

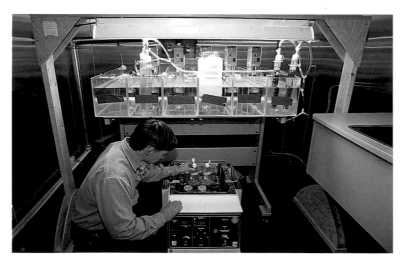

The main U.S. Antarctic base at McMurdo Station is managed by the National Science Foundation. The new Crary Science Lab (*above*), completed in 1992 at a cost of $25 million, has controlled laboratory cold rooms. Rumors circulated that spending tax dollars on refrigerators in Antarctica made it a candidate for Senator Proxmire's "Golden Fleece Award," but the immediate result was a higher standard of polar field research. A cold room enables Dr. Sean Turner (*left*) to culture cold-adapted algae from local rocks and to utilize the latest techniques of molecular biology to look for unique sequences in DNA and enzymes. Dr. Charles Knight (*right*) of the National Center for Atmospheric Research uses another cold room to study polarized ice crystals to better understand how natural anti-freezes prevent nonsalty fluids from crystallizing in fish that live in seawater below 32°F. Rod Rozier (*far right*) launches a balloon carrying a $30,000 instrument package to test stratospheric ozone levels, which drastically drop at certain elevations during the first weeks of spring. He believes that we all should take serious note of the clear evidence that what we have done in the temperate latitudes has affected Antarctica, but he is far less certain that the ozone hole over Antarctica will significantly affect our future.

Eskimo Subsistence Whaling

Eskimo whaling captain Thomas Brower III (*above*), in a sealskin umiak, sits motionless by an open lead in the frozen Arctic Ocean off Barrow, Alaska, waiting for a bowhead whale (an endangered species) to surface (*right, above*). Though he had been whaling for over thirty years since he was a child, he harpooned his first whale in 1994 right beside me (*see page 70*). Forty crews were hunting on a strict quota system based on the number of strikes of the harpoon rather than on the number of landed whales. His whale was only the second of the year. During the week I spent on the ice with him, he pushed off his umiak with a crew of five numerous times toward whales that breached within 30 feet of us, raised his harpoon, but didn't throw it until conditions were perfect: the odds of a poor strike or of losing a whale under the ice were too great. After the harpoon stuck and the whale was dispatched as humanely as possible with a special bomb gun (*see page 66*), he landed the whale with the help of all able-bodied hands from his village (*right*). Within hours, they had fully butchered the whale (*far right, above*) and taken it home, leaving only scraps on the skeleton for a polar bear that appeared the next morning.

Historic Huts of the Heroic Age

The stocked huts of several great Antarctic explorers are quite literally frozen in time. Robert Falcon Scott never made it back to his hut at Cape Evans (*left*). After being beaten to the South Pole in 1911 by Roald Amundsen (whose hut, built on an ice shelf, soon vanished), Scott died on his return trip. Original chemicals in Scott's science lab (*above*) are as intact in their bottles as the naturally freeze-dried emperor penguin on the nearby desk of Edward Wilson (*right, above*), who brought the penguin back from "the worst journey in the world" (*see pages 92–93*). Ernest Shackleton did return to his 1907 hut at Cape Royds with all his men after deciding, just 97 nautical miles from the pole, that "a live donkey is better than a dead lion." His hut still contains jars of food (*far right*), as well as a British newspaper (*right*), unyellowed with age, that advertises a 24-day cruise to Scandinavia for £6 sterling (about $10 U.S.).

Up and around Mount McKinley

The most condemning evidence against Frederick Cook's poorly documented claim to have reached the North Pole in 1908 before Robert Peary was his false first ascent of Mount McKinley (*second left, above*) two years earlier. Experts proved that his summit photograph of the 20,320-foot highest peak in the polar regions was bogus and doubted that he could have climbed the peak in just a few days. Cook had, however, made a genuine 540-mile, four-month circumnavigation of the peak in 1903 that went unrepeated for seventy-five years.

In 1978, Olympic skier Ned Gillette and I dreamed up two related adventures. Starting in late winter with Alan Bard and Doug Weins (*far left*), we spent nineteen days in extreme Arctic conditions circling the peak on skis within the limits of its glacier systems. Then Ned and I attempted the first one-day ascent of the mountain, failing on our first try because of a fall, but succeeding on our second a month later. We started one evening from 10,000-foot Kahiltna Pass between the peak and Mount Foraker, climbing through the undark night (*second left, below*), past alpenglow on corniced ridges (*left*), to reach the summit during the day. After a short bivouac on the descent, we continued down on skis (*below*).

The World's Southernmost Active Volcano

Mount Erebus rises 12,447 feet directly out of the Ross Sea of Antarctica (*left*), a greater vertical distance than Mount Everest above its base camp. The summit crater (*above*) has one of only three known continuously molten lava lakes, hidden beneath vapors rising from 800 feet below the rim. The tiny figure on the rim in the upper right of this image provides a sense of scale. Members of Shackleton's South Pole expedition, who made the first ascent of the peak in 1908, commented on "the extraordinary structures which rose every here and there" around the crater rim. Wild towers of steaming ice (*far right, below; see also page 87*) are created by freezing vapors from hot fumaroles. I spent six days in 1992 with Tim Cully exploring and photographing the most fascinating mountain summit I have ever visited. We rappelled 85 feet into one of the towers (*right*), instantly moving from 30°F below zero to 30°F above zero. At the bottom were dark catacombs, with floors of black lava and roofs of giant ice crystals old enough to boost our confidence in the stability of the place. After climbing out on our ropes, we traversed a wild landscape of convoluted windblown snow called *sastrugi* (*far right, above*) back to a science hut at 11,000 feet.

A Closer Look at Polar Bears

A yearling cub (*above*) cuddles against his mother who has been tranquilized from a helicopter with a dart gun. As biologist Susan Polischuk approaches, the cub unexpectedly charges (*right, above*) past a second dart on a probe but fortuitously stops short. The cub is netted (*right, below*) and weighed in at 250 pounds in a scene reminiscent of *Little Red Riding Hood*. Polischuk and fellow researchers (*far right*) test both bears' vital signs before monitoring toxic contamination of the mother's milk and aspects of their metabolism. At the end of the summer, when body fat is lowest, levels of PCBs and other organochlorines may be high enough to rate polar bear milk unfit for human consumption, although greater risks might be involved in procuring enough to become contaminated. Toxic chemicals from sources thousands of miles away bioaccumulate in Arctic animals and

reach their zenith in top predators of marine ecosystems. Toxics can arrive directly in seawater or from dirty air generated by northern cities that becomes Arctic haze (*see page 82*), which drops particles into the sea where they are absorbed by phytoplanktons that are eaten by fish that are eaten by seals that are eaten by polar bears and people. A study of breast milk in Canadian Inuit women who regularly ate seal blubber found alarming concentrations of PCBs and DDT metabolites, four to seven times greater than in women who did not. Life at the top of the food chain has taken on a new meaning, adding a touch of sadness to these eloquent words written by bear researcher Ian Stirling: "The wild polar bear is the Arctic incarnate . . . not just a symbol but the very embodiment of life in the Arctic."

107

The Exemplary Emperor

Emperor penguins are the only warm-blooded creatures that winter and breed so far south. Their survival on the sea ice at the edge of the Antarctic continent depends on total cooperation and lack of conspecific aggression. They offer a model for human society to emulate as we elbow each other in increasingly crowded, hostile breeding colonies set in ever-less-friendly environments of our own making. An emperor walking toward its colony on the fast ice beside the Weddell Sea (*far right*) may weigh over 60 pounds, with its belly full of fish for its hungry chick. After days or months at sea, it sings a haunting, ventriloquial call, with a unique voiceprint, to find its mate in a colony of thousands. A greeting ritual (*right*) reconfirms the pair bond in the heart of the colony (*above*) before food is regurgitated to a chick (*left*), who is unable to forage in the sea until it molts. Emperors survive the winter by huddling in tight clusters that appear at first glance to be stationary. Warm birds slowly give up their places to colder neighbors on the windward edge. During the two coldest months, the females forage at sea while the males stay home and incubate the single egg, which is held on their toes and protected by a special fold of skin.

Wrangel Island

Surrounded by pack ice that breaks up only in the summer (*right, above*), Wrangel Island provides ideal habitat for the Arctic's largest population of denning polar bears. Human numbers are far lower at the Russian science base and only village of Ushakovskoye (*right*), where scientists and transplanted Siberian natives (*far right*) live side by side. The metaphor of Wrangel as the Galápagos of the North goes beyond abundant wildlife on uninhabited islands. Discoveries here, like clues on the Galápagos for Darwin, are causing long-accepted beliefs to be revised. The mammoth was believed to have become extinct at the close of the Pleistocene 10,000 years ago as a consequence of climate change, but Sergey Vartanyan (*left*) holds teeth he found in 1992 from a mammoth that walked the Wrangel tundra in about 1600 B.C., well after the dawn of civilization. Survival of mammoths so far north on an island where there were no humans adds credence to the idea that Arctic hunters dealt the final blows to the mainland mammoth, as they did more recently to another vestige of the ice age, the musk ox (*above*), which disappeared from Europe and Asia at least 2,000 years ago, but from Alaska only in 1865. Musk oxen from Greenland stock bred in Alaska that were transplanted to Wrangel in 1975 are doing well.

South Georgia Island

Despite centuries of relentless exploitation by sealers and whalers, South Georgia Island still has the Southern Ocean's largest concentration of wildlife. Over a million king penguins breed beneath the glacier-draped peaks of the interior of the island. While some penguins stand around on the tundra of the Salisbury Plain (*above*), others sleep (*left*) on their heels with heads tucked down and eggs held on their toes. Between the founding of the Norwegian whaling town of Grytviken (*right, above*) in 1904 and the end of World War I, 175,000 whales were killed. The station was abandoned in 1965 for economic, rather than environmental, reasons. Early in the nineteenth century up to a million Antarctic fur seals (*right*) were killed each year, until by 1820 they were scarce and by 1900 they seemed to be completely decimated. From a few survivors discovered on an offshore island in the 1930s, however, the South Georgia population has increased to more than 2 million. The huge Southern Ocean Whale Sanctuary, created in 1994 by the International Whaling Commission, includes South Georgia, but its success remains uncertain because pirate ships from Japan and Russia openly defy the ban.

A Polar Bear and a Sled Dog

At a remote camp several miles outside Churchill, I watched a bear walk directly toward a barking sled dog (*right, above*) with an utter calm that an armed human might easily mistake for aggression. Instead, the bear rubbed noses with the dog, bowled him over gently with a huge paw, and began to play (*above, and far right, above*). The dog leapt up and responded much the way a pup does to a parent. They played with amazing restraint for half an hour, until the superbly insulated bear overheated and sat down not far from our truck, ignoring us. Later, a Manitoba game warden, making his rounds, stopped to monitor "our" bear and two others in the area. One of the bears came up to the bed of the warden's truck to sniff traces of seal meat used to bait mechanical bear traps. With this evidence of its potential threat to human safety, the warden shot all three bears, including the one we had watched (*right*), with tranquilizer darts. One bear with a prior record of investigating human food sources was euthanized, while "our" bear was put in "polar bear jail," a holding facility that provides negative experiences to bears that approach human food sources. When pack ice formed on Hudson Bay a few weeks later and the bear was released, it instantly headed out to hunt seals.

115

Antarctic Biology

Where two geologists (*right*) walking in the Trans-antarctic Mountains above the Dry Valleys see a lifeless boundary between sediments and volcanics, biologists have discovered a faint stripe of crypto-endolithic life growing under the surface of sand-stones. These microscopic plants can be cultured in the laboratory (*second right, below*). Freshwater algae (*far right, below*) growing in frozen Lake Hoare are studied by desert biologist Bob Wharton.

A "dedicated" Weddell seal (*second right, above*) has been captured and released into a hole drilled in the sea ice, miles from the seal's natural hole, by Warren Zapol's team of doctors. Every 30 to 90 minutes the seal pops up for air into a heated and furnished National Science Foundation hut erected over the hole, complete with beds and stereo music. While the seal takes long breaths, the men plug the wire on its back into a computer to download data from a tiny laser implant that monitors blood-oxygen levels. Other devices measure velocity, depth, pulse, and respiration. The overall goal is to better understand the rapid "dive response" that allows this mammal to avoid problems humans have when they stop breathing for far shorter periods or attempt far shallower dives. The live, beating heart (*far right, above*) of an Antarctic cod is studied in McMurdo's new Crary Science Lab by Ting Wang in an effort to understand how the cod survives in 28°F seawater and why its heart stops beating at temperatures above 46°F.

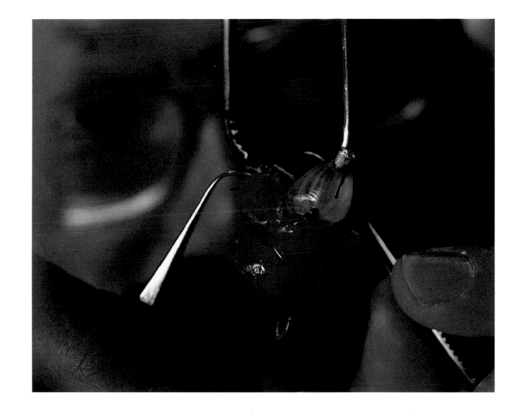

Cirque of the Unclimbables

In a remote valley of the Logan Mountains of Canada's Northwest Territories, wild granite spires erupt out of lush, treeless meadows. When I first climbed in the Cirque in 1972 and 1973, fewer than twenty-five people had ever visited the simplified subarctic landscape of this paradise on Earth. Moss campion (*far left, below*) clings to the rock and flowers in the brief summer. My partner, Jim McCarthy, had climbed the most sheer face on Mount Proboscis (*second left*) back in 1963, a first ascent that went unrepeated for thirty years. I returned in 1993 with Todd Skinner (*far left, above*) and Paul Piana (*below*). Their free ascent of Yosemite's El Capitan five years earlier had yet to be repeated, and the new route we chose up Proboscis proved to be harder—the most continuously difficult free climbing yet done on a mountain face. Our final bivouac atop the knife-edged summit ridge (*below*) was spent with feet dangling off one side and heads off the other. But it was mercifully short; we had climbed well past midnight under a nearly full moon (*left*).

In Shackleton's Wake

Until 1993, Antarctic tourist ships avoided the Weddell Sea (*above*), where Shackleton's ship, the *Endurance*, was crushed by pack ice in 1915, in waters where miles-wide tabular icebergs (*right*) are a common sight. In one of the greatest survival epics in history, Shackleton spent a year and a half leading all twenty-eight members of his handpicked team to safety after he gave up his goal of traversing Antarctica over the South Pole. In an open boat only 5 feet wide, he sailed the final 750 miles to South Georgia across the world's roughest seas.

Barbara and I joined the first tourist voyage deep into the Weddell Sea aboard the *Kapitan Khlebnikov* (*far right, above*), a Russian icebreaker outfitted with helicopters and Zodiac rafts that we launched (*right, above*) to visit islands on what turned out to be one of the world's finest wildlife itineraries. Like Shackleton, we saw emperor penguins that live and breed only at extreme latitudes much farther south than the relatively temperate peninsula visited by most cruises. We also saw the world's largest penguin colony, of chinstraps, on the remote South Sandwich Islands. When we reached South Georgia, we toasted Shackleton at his grave (*left*), near where he died at sea on a later journey.

Northeast Greenland National Park

A crack team of specially trained Danish soldiers, called the Sirius Sled Patrol, travels in pairs by dogsled for months at a time monitoring the coastal perimeter of the world's largest national park, which includes most of northern Greenland and extends 12 miles offshore. Their heavy sleds pull more efficiently with dogs harnessed in an Eskimo-style fan (*above*), instead of in the more familiar pairings used for trails through wooded country. One soldier often needs to run ahead to guide the dogs around obstacles and to check out the safety of the sea ice. Part of the soldiers' training is to run the Copenhagen Marathon just before departing for a two-year tour of duty that blends the roles of border guard, park ranger, and game warden. Nights with the northern lights dancing across the sky (*far right*) are spent in special tents anchored to the sled. Lars Ulsoe (*right, above*) hugs his lead dog, Charlie, who has been raised with love and affection from specially bred Greenland Eskimo sled dog stock. Wild mammals of the uninhabited northeast coast have little fear of humans, but attacks are quite uncommon. Scuffling sounds outside the tent and visions of white animals moving in the moonlight are far more likely to be Arctic hares (*right*) than polar bears.

The Antarctic Sahara

The improbable sands of the Dry Valleys (*above*) are aberrant clues that the Antarctic continent is a cold desert. The bones of the landscape stand out in ice-free silence where the Transantarctic Mountains of southern Victoria Land have blocked the outward flow of the polar ice sheet. Millions of years of wind-driven ice and gravel have sculpted so many holes and jug handles into the steep walls of hard rock (*far right*) that I could casually climb them unroped with gloves on. Not a blade of grass or an insect survives on a moonscape where it may not have rained since the end of the Pleistocene. Frost-heaved "patterned ground" (*right, above*) etched by a dusting of snow holds a false sense of intentional design in a place apart from the evolution of intelligent life. The eerie pointing finger (*right*) belongs to a mummy seal that crawled inland thousands of years ago only to die "with a sudden, horrible misunderstanding of geography," in the words of polar author Barry Lopez, who acutely sensed the "monumental indifference" of this land to human existence. Nearby Mummy Pond (*left*) is an equally improbable lake of liquid water covered by at least 9 feet of ice year round. Blood Fall (*second right, above*) is a cascade of ice and reddish mineral salts leached over time from the surrounding rocks.

125

The Siberian Coast

The pristine tundra of a Russian nature preserve on Arakamchechen Island (*above*) contrasts with appalling impact, elsewhere on Siberian Arctic shores, on what has been called "the Earth's most fragile biome." While some Chukchi Inuit (*left; far right, above*) herd reindeer in timeless fashion, others add a modern spin to the word "timeless," as uncontrolled use of demilitarized tracked vehicles scars the landscape (*right*). This Chukchi tank driver (*right, above*), almost too drunk to walk, caroms across the tundra on his way back from a traditional festival. The buildings in the distance are government farms where foxes are raised for fur. Each village is required to supply a quota of wild walrus and whale meat to feed the thousands of animals. Since the 1991 breakup of the Soviet Union, Siberian wildlands, whether protected or not, have suffered rapid resource exploitation by a desperate population suddenly torn both from its former socio-economic umbrella and from enforcement of environmental regulations. Despite bright spots, such as the creation in 1993 of a 10-million-acre Great Arctic Preserve in the eastern sector of the north coast of Siberia, the larger question throughout the Arctic is whether subsistence cultures in daily contact with high-tech modern life can survive into the future with their traditions even somewhat intact.

The Antarctic Peninsula

Cruising between Antarctic peaks and glaciers (*right*) gave me the impression of floating at more than 20,000 feet through the high Himalaya after a flood far greater than the one reported in the Bible had raised the level of the oceans. The difference was that, despite the region's overwhelming pristine nature, signs of human intrusions stood out wherever boats could be landed—none of them caused by tourists. A gentoo penguin (*far right, below*) sat on a rusting drum amidst the derelict buildings, machinery, toxic wastes, and just plain rubbish of an abandoned Chilean science base. The hull of the *Bahia Paraiso* (*above*) bobbed where it had spilled 170,000 gallons of diesel oil in 1989, 2 miles from the U.S. Palmer Station. Although widely reported as a tourist vessel, the Argentine ship's primary mission was resupplying science bases, such as Esperanza Station, where even in 1993 fresh trash was still being thrown into the sea (*left*). We were able to swim in Antarctic seawater without wet suits (*far right, above*) at a geothermal area within the flooded crater of Deception Island, a natural harbor badly littered by whalers and scientists who left in haste as recently as 1969, when a major volcanic eruption began.

North Pole by Nuclear Icebreaker

The North Pole (*above*) is in the middle of the Arctic Ocean, where there are frequent open leads of water. Barbara and I arrived in 1993 aboard the Russian icebreaker *Yamal* (*left, above*), which is powered by a nuclear reactor (*left*). After passengers and crew danced a circle through all twenty-four time zones and drank toasts, I wanted to photograph the ship's GPS (global positioning satellite) readout at the pole, which I had seen forty minutes earlier. To my surprise (*far left*), it showed us to be a mile from the pole. As indicated by the SOG (speed over ground) readout, the ship was drifting imperceptibly at 1.5 knots (1.7 mph) along with the vast expanse of seemingly motionless pack ice.

   Both the crew and staff of the *Yamal* doubted Peary's claim that he reached the vicinity of the pole using solar latitude readings uncorrected by longitude data. One of our two captains, who had made six of the eleven successful surface voyages to the pole since 1977, remarked on having just seen the sun near the pole for the first time. On our return trip we responded to a call from a diesel icebreaker that was trapped in pack ice off the north coast of Greenland with a hundred tourists aboard. Among the staff lecturers was Wally Herbert (*right*), almost certainly the first person to reach the North Pole by nonmotorized means during an epic year-and-a-half trans-Arctic traverse in 1969.

Science at the South Pole

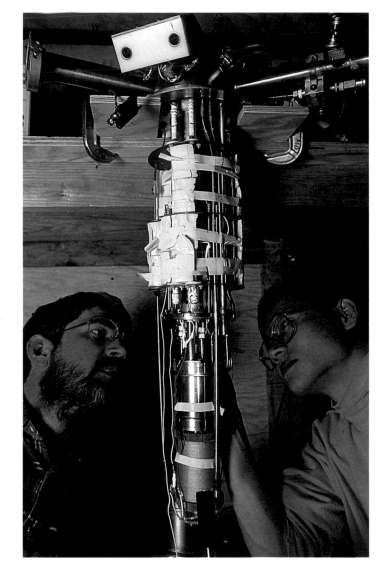

After Scott reached the pole a month behind Amundsen in early 1912, the next visitors came by air in 1956 to establish a U.S. research station for the International Geophysical Year. Continuously occupied since 1957, the pole has become a prime site for atmospheric and astrophysical science in clear air and dry cold at 9,300 feet, where instruments are never subjected to rain or corrosion. A solar parhelion (*left, above*) refracts from falling ice crystals, called "diamond dust," that surround sensors for astrophysical gamma ray sources. Jeff Peterson and Hien Nguyen (*above right*) create greater cold in an effort to detect the seeds of structure of the Universe in patterns of cosmic radiation released soon after the Big Bang. They assemble a device to cool a detector to .05°C (.09°F) above absolute zero to attain superconductivity. In contrast, vegetables growing in a greenhouse at 80°F (*left*) make life more pleasant during the eight months of isolation when the station has no flights. My self-portrait at the pole (*far left, below*) on a balmy -45°F spring day shows yearly survey markers 30 feet apart receding into the distance atop moving glacial ice. Steve Warren (*above*), who in 1992 became the most senior scientist to winter over, with twenty-one other souls in temperatures dropping below -100°F, often climbed this 70-foot metal tower to obtain virgin snow samples for climatic research.

133

A Modern Eskimo Winter

When the sun drops below pressure ridges on the frozen Chukchi Sea (*above*) one late November afternoon in Barrow, Alaska, it doesn't rise again for sixty-seven days. Residents of this most northerly town of the United States don't exactly crawl into their igloos, even though Barrow used to be a sleepy Inupiat Eskimo village. Contrary to legend, Alaskan Eskimos never used igloos, except as temporary, tentlike shelters for winter travels. After the completion of the Trans-Alaska Pipeline, property taxes on oilfield equipment transformed Barrow into the world's richest municipality, with not only a higher average income than Kuwait or Beverly Hills, but also more elaborate social services. Inside America's most expensive elementary school, which cost $62.5 million to build, is a giant year-round playground (*right*). Many children still play outdoors on fine winter days (*left; far right*). Eskimo families generally live in modest homes (*right, above*), investing their net worth in their native corporations and community in a visionary effort to preserve their subsistence culture in harmony with an advanced technological society. So many outside engineers, scientists, and doctors have been hired by the North Slope Borough and the regional native corporations that nonnatives now account for 40 percent of the 3,500 residents.

Downtown Mac Town, Antarctica

On a moonlit spring evening seen from miles out on the frozen Ross Sea against the 12,447-foot rise of Mount Erebus, the major U.S. research station in Antarctica (*far right, above*) appears like a fairy-tale town. A closer look (*second right, below*) reveals a disappointing extension of contemporary America. Wires, pipes, and buildings seem to erupt randomly from the land. Inside, appearances are much better (*far right, below*), as in this National Science Foundation meeting room. After a controversial open dump was closed in 1991, recycling at twice the standard of the most efficient U.S. city (*above*) was instituted for the town's 1,600 summer occupants. Mountains of compacted cans now await yearly export by ship. Major changes are on a slower clock. Architects have begun long-range planning for a more efficient and aesthetic McMurdo, one that can coexist for centuries alongside the natural "clean rooms" (*right*) that brought science to the pristine global laboratory of Antarctica in the first place. The question remains whether science and tourism will be able to continuously use the polar regions without harming their potential to reveal changes on Earth, as well as clues to its past history.

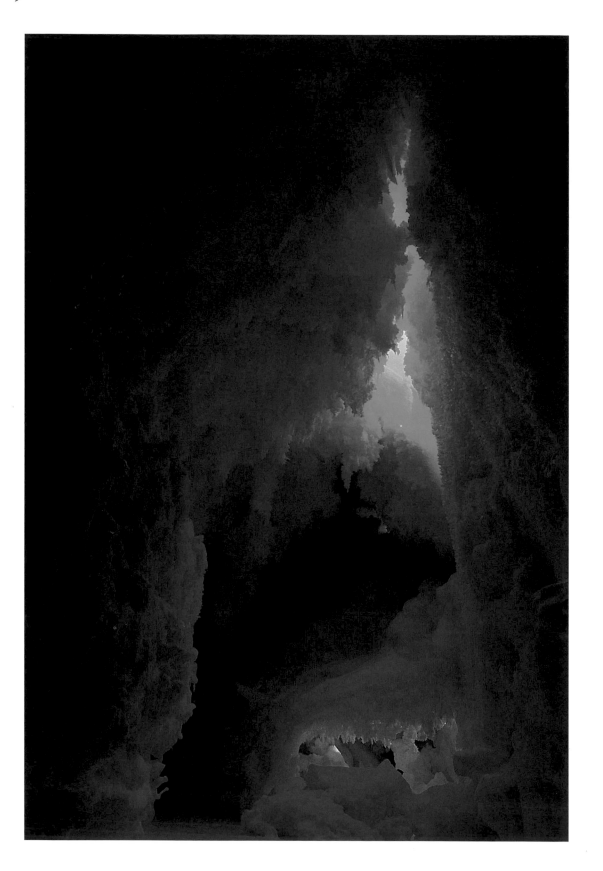

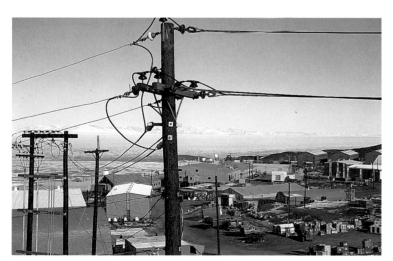

Part Three: Essays about the Photographs

Sculpture at annual Ice Festival, Fairbanks, Alaska; 1994 *p. 7, 89, 139*
Fairbanks locals advised me to photograph the winter Ice Festival in the evening when special lighting gives eye-popping colors to ice sculptures carved by artists from around the world. As I began long exposures to capture the vivid reds, greens, and purples, I questioned what I would ever do with these images. They did not fit with the theme of my polar book, nor did they reflect my personal ethic of using photography to see the world more deeply through the visual language of film without introducing things that aren't really out there simply to draw the viewer's eye.

Of course I could always say the lights were already there, but if I avoided using colored filters to create phony sunsets and double-exposing skies and moons to assemble scenes that might have been but really weren't, what was I doing photographing ice in garish artificial lighting?

I listened to my intuition, unsure where it would lead me, and returned on a cloudy day when the park beside the Chena River was nearly empty and the ice had a natural bluish cast. I singled out just the head of a larger-than-life figure against a dark wall and shot a full roll, trying to find the correct angle on the face in combination with kaleidoscopic sky reflections on the cheeks and around the eyes. These reflections changed radically by moving the camera just half an inch. The sculpture's contours had begun to soften in the sun. Focusing on the face emphasized an emergent abstractness that had not been apparent under contrasty lights. Thus a complex form on a pedestal in a city was reduced to a simple metaphor for human activity in the wild polar regions. *(Nikon F4, 80–200mm f2.8 lens, f16 at 1/2 second, Fuji Velvia)*

Mist over the John River at sunrise near Gates of the Arctic National Park, Brooks Range, Alaska; 1993 *p. 8*
While flying into Gates of the Arctic to photograph the wild granite spires of the Arrigetch Range, I saw the first light of dawn catch an undulating veil of mist hanging over the John River. It had begun to spread and dissipate over the boreal forest, and I knew it would last a few brief minutes at best. Vern Kingsford, the pilot of the single-engine Cessna 172, circled down and made repeated passes over the mist while I opened a window and framed a number of different compositions. At first I used a telephoto to emphasize the shafts of light coming up through a tight group of trees, but I could feel that the shot wasn't working, because the line of the edge of the river overpowered the subtle light beams I wanted to capture. The image also seemed a bit too abstract and disconnected from the broader sense of the wild Arctic I wanted to communicate. The central trees and mist by themselves lacked context, much like an animal portrait taken in a zoo rather than in a broader, wild landscape.

I decided to use the arcs of the river running through a large area of mist in magical light as the focal point of my composition. As Vern kept circling, I switched to a wider lens and tried to make the river's path appear as long, diagonal, and random as possible, while preserving the quality of light that had first drawn me and convinced us to abort our direct flight path to the spires of the Arrigetch Range. *(Nikon F4, 35mm f1.4 lens, f1.4 at 1/1000 second, Fuji Velvia push processed to ISO 100)*

King penguin colony at Saint Andrews Bay, South Georgia Island, Subantarctic; 1993 *p. 9*
After I had disembarked from the Russian icebreaker *Kapitan Khlebnikov* beside a breeding colony of king penguins, I rushed to a hilltop to get some overview shots before some of the other 107 passengers stepped into the scene. I knew I would be able to focus in on individual penguins or small groups of them later on. As I began composing this picture, I wanted to create the feeling of an endless number of birds by trying to have tightly clustered penguins spilling off all four sides. At the same time I felt the foreground edge shouldn't just randomly cut penguins in half. The photo needed some logic to it that showed personal vision, rather than being just a snapshot. Something felt strangely familiar as I tried to compose one section of birds to symbolize the broader scene before me, which had at least twenty times as many birds and a river running through it. In my mind's eye, I saw a potential graphic similarity between the boreal forest split by a stream I had photographed a few months before in the Far North and the penguin forest split by a stream before me now. I evolved this composition by remembering how the line of the river cut through the forest in my previous photo and by not including other photographers who were now amidst the penguins just to the left of this scene. With my camera on a tripod, I carefully framed the scene to favor more dark chicks along the leading edge and to break at the lower right corner with a pair of adults crossing beaks. I returned other times throughout the day, but the scene never looked as good as in those first minutes. *(Nikon F4, 80–200mm f2.8 lens, f16 at 1/2 second, Fuji Velvia)*

Dog team in winter on the frozen Arctic Ocean near Barrow, Alaska; 1994 *p. 10*
Geoff Carroll runs his dog team on a -25°F winter evening on the sea ice of the Arctic Ocean near his home in Barrow, Alaska. His team is one of the last few in an Eskimo village that began switching to snowmobiles in the sixties. Geoff doesn't care if machines can be parked and not fed until the next winter; he likes dogs and makes them an important part of his life. In 1986, he ran a team of this same breed of Eskimo sled dog to the North Pole on a journey with Will Steger of Minnesota that was later featured in *National Geographic*. A biologist formerly involved with endangered bowhead whales, Geoff now works for the Alaska Department of Fish and Game, managing the land mammals and birds of a major portion of the North Slope of the Brooks Range.

To make this photograph, I asked Geoff to drop me off from his sled in a broad, smooth area on the pack ice between pressure ridges. A few minutes before sunset, I set up my camera on a tripod while Geoff cut circles on the ice with his team. A special Singh-Ray two-stop graduated neutral-density filter helped balance the exposure between the bright red sky and the weaker blue of the pack ice without altering the natural color balance. *(Nikon F4, 80–200mm f2.8 lens, f4 at 1/125 second, Fuji Velvia push processed to ISO 100)*

Looking across the frozen Ross Sea from the summit of Mount Erebus to the Transantarctic Mountains; 1992 *p. 11*

National Science Foundation survival guide Tim Cully gazes down 12,447 feet from the world's most southerly active volcano to sea level at McMurdo Sound in the early Antarctic spring. Tim's breath forms a halo of mist around his face at -32°F on a rare windless night. The sun is far enough above the horizon that in most years it would not have created diffuse pink sky colors. As more of a point source in a blue sky, the sunlight would have been too harsh to make either this photograph or the ice towers on pages 87 and 105. The "Pinatubo effect," which was created by the huge eruption of the equatorial volcano the previous year, caused the broad area of warm color around the sun that sets off Tim's figure.

In clear Antarctic air, distances are far greater than they appear. The 12,447-foot drop from Mount Erebus to the sea ice is about 1,000 feet greater than that from the top of Mount Everest to its base camp. The Transantarctic Mountains are more than 70 miles away. I spent six nights—sleeping by day—exploring the upper reaches of the volcano with Tim. I kept photographing with an electronic camera in extreme conditions by paying attention to details on both sides of the critical human/machine interface. I felt as comfortable as skiing from a chairlift when I handheld my camera for this photograph in deerskin mittens with Grabber handwarmer packs and polypro inner gloves. Use of autofocus and autoexposure minimized use of fingers except where manual settings were really needed. Battery power came from a warm remote pack in my shirt pocket attached to the camera with a wire. *(Nikon F4, 24mm f2.8 lens, f11 at 1/30 second, Fuji Velvia)*

Sunrise over raised pressure ridges in Youngsund Fjord, Northeast Greenland National Park; 1993 *p. 12*

Here at latitude 74° north in the world's largest national park, alpenglow at dawn has just touched sea level. For the moment, snow on the terrestrial mountains is pink, while foreground sea ice reflects the rich blue of the sky. I make it a point to search out special times and places where natural edges of light and form will coincide. A few minutes later, the entire landscape assumed an overall bluish cast. Textures in the sea ice become especially graphic soon after it first freezes in October. Until fresh snow buries the contours, raised fragments of tidal pressure ridges stand out in bold relief. I chose this one because it was set within an arc of just-frozen surface water atop 6 inches of slightly older ice thick enough to cross with our dogsled.

I was traveling with members of the Sirius Sled Patrol (see pages 122–23), a Danish military team that each winter patrols thousands of miles of coastline in northern Greenland. Teams of two spend a month or more at a time with their dogs out monitoring conditions in the park and maintaining a legal presence in these vast, uninhabited sections of the country.

To make this image, I was out well before dawn to look for a place where the lines of the ice would lead my viewer's eye through the scene to the sunrise glow on the peaks. I used a Singh-Ray two-stop graduated neutral-density filter to hold an exposure for the sunlit peaks without having the shadowed blue ice go too dark. I set my camera on a large tripod and further maximized sharpness from foreground to background by using a wide-angle lens set at a small aperture. *(Nikon F4, 20mm f4 lens, f16 at 1/4 second, Fuji Velvia)*

Midnight sun on Mount Erebus over raised pressure ridges in sea ice, Ross Island, Antarctica; 1992 *p. 13*

This photograph depicts neither sunrise nor sunset as we know it. Night has fallen on McMurdo Sound in the frozen Ross Sea, while crimson light bathes Mount Erebus, where 24 hour daylight had already arrived high on the peak in mid-October, a week before it reached sea level. The summit that appears to rise just behind the sea-level ice is actually 30 miles away in the incredibly clear air. Alpenglow in the temperate latitudes disappears after an evanescent couple of minutes, yet here the icy peak glowed shades of red during the entire three-hour night as the tide-fractured sea ice in the foreground held a soft bluish green in the never-dark shadows. I used a two-stop graduated neutral-density filter to produce an even exposure, close to how the eye sees it, between pink sunlight above and blue shadow below.

I made this image on a tripod at midnight about 2 miles from McMurdo Station, the main United States science base on the continent. In 1840, the great explorer Sir James Clark Ross named Mount Erebus after his lead ship and McMurdo Sound after one of his lieutenants. Geographers later added his own name to the sea and the Ross Ice Shelf, a Texas-sized 200-foot-thick sheet of glacial ice that floats on the sea south of Ross Island. Below Mount Erebus near its edge lies the most southerly land anchorage in the world, accessible by ship only during the month or two when the seasonal pack ice has melted. The great explorers Robert Falcon Scott and Ernest Shackleton built huts here early in the 1900s for their attempts to reach the South Pole. *(Nikon F4, 85mm f2 lens, f16 at 1/2 second, Fuji Velvia)*

Caribou near the Killik River, Gates of the Arctic National Park, Alaska; 1993 *p. 14*

To photograph so many locations for this book, I used every scheme I could dream up beyond assignments, grants, tour leading, and frequent-flier miles. This image resulted from horse-trading a photo workshop to an Alaskan bush pilot for future services. My wife, Barbara, used some of our time with Vern Kingsford to get her FAA floatplane rating; we also did several days of aerial photography north of the Arctic Circle in the Brooks Range. In August, no large groups of caribou were migrating, but we did spot smaller groups moving through the valley of the Killik River. When a rainbow suddenly appeared, my best shot held only a hint of its lower edge behind distant animals. As we climbed up again, we spotted seven wolves around a den. When I exclaimed about our incredible luck to have so much happening in one spot, Barbara said, "All we need now is a grizzly!" Within the minute a grizzly stood up in front of the plane on the tundra and charged off toward the very surprised caribou. I opened the window of the plane and used a fast f1.4 telephoto to hold a high shutter speed as we flew over the fleeing animals. Some frames showed the grizzly in the distance, but this one is my favorite because it evokes the feeling of an Arctic Serengeti. Compared with images of larger herds in the more barren landscapes of the spring and fall migrations, this small group on the run surrounded by endless summer greenery presents a more distinctive contrast to the opposing image of penguins on ice. *(Nikon F4, 85mm f1.4 lens, f1.4 at 1/4000 second, Fuji Velvia push processed to ISO 100)*

141

Chinstrap penguins on an iceberg, South Sandwich Islands, Subantarctic; 1993 *p. 15*

While on a Russian icebreaker heading north toward the end of the first tourist expedition into the Weddell Sea by ship, we visited the remote South Sandwich Islands in typically stormy weather. We passed Candlemas Island, a perfectly shaped active volcano rising out of the sea, but were unable to land Zodiac rafts because of rough seas. As we were heading for Zavadovsky Island, which has about 12 million chinstrap penguins in the world's largest penguin rookery, we spotted an especially vivid blue berg of glacial ice with a few hundred chinstrap penguins clinging to its sides. We headed out for several miles in the Zodiacs, but the seas were so rough near the berg that I didn't dare take out my standard Nikon gear from a waterproof bag. In dim light with a small underwater camera that had a rather slow lens, I tried photographing a leopard seal lying in wait for a penguin to slip off the berg, reasonably sure that the result wouldn't be sharp enough to publish. With the swells running 10 feet and tipping the raft near the sloping ice, I waited to use my Nikon until we were well away from the wash of the berg. Then I set my *f*1.4 85mm lens wide open to hold a fast-enough shutter speed to produce one sharp frame out of about ten tries, shooting only at the stillest moment when the raft's rocking motion changed from up to down. *(Nikon F4, 85mm f1.4 lens, f1.4 at 1/250 second, Fuji Velvia pushed one stop to ISO 100)*

Polar bear with cubs-of-the-year in a blizzard on the shore of Hudson Bay, Canada; 1993 *p. 16*

Churchill, Manitoba, is the best place to see large numbers of polar bears. In the fall, just before Cape Churchill attracts the first pack ice in Hudson Bay, more than 300 bears gather onshore, waiting to head out for the winter and hunt seals the moment the ice forms. Backpacking is not advised because of the danger of the bears and the extreme climate. Guided group tours on special tundra buggies offer good viewing, but compromised photography. Barbara and I opted for Donnie Wolkowski's fat-tired but far smaller photo bus so that we could choose our own locations, shoot low from a bear's perspective, and avoid the shaking that always happens in a larger group vehicle.

Thus we were able to experience a remarkable day in the life of a mother and two small cubs. When we spotted them at dawn, hunkered down in the lee of a beached block of sea ice, we decided to stay with them as long as possible. Mothers with young rarely frequent areas near so many adult males who might attack and kill the cubs (thus increasing their ability to contribute to the gene pool by bringing the female into estrus). I was positioned with 600mm of lens firmly set on a tripod and aimed out the open window of our vehicle. Hours passed with little movement from the bears; then suddenly she would be up and moving, scouting the area and leading her cubs to a new resting place. At the moment of this photograph, I caught the cubs tightly flanking their mother for safety and protection from the fierce winds. Less than a minute later, they vanished into the whiteness. *(Nikon F4, 300mm f2.8 AFI lens with 2X teleconverter for 600mm, f5.6 at 1/60 second, Fuji Velvia push processed to ISO 100)*

Emperor penguin chicks in a blizzard, Riiser-Larsen Ice Shelf, Weddell Sea, Antarctica; 1993 *p. 17*

Emperor penguins winter on the edge of the main Antarctic continent, far to the south of the Antarctic Peninsula, where most cruises visit. During the first tourist voyage into the Weddell Sea aboard a Russian icebreaker, we located this colony by ship-based helicopter. A blizzard prevented further flights to land passengers near the colony, and the ice edge was too high to land Zodiac rafts. In the great tradition of all things big, powerful, and Russian, the captain rammed his 800-ton vessel firmly into the pack ice. We simply stepped off and walked a mile into the wild conditions that these birds regularly experience. They survive through extreme mutual cooperation. In late winter, young chicks and adults form tight huddles for warmth without fear that some bad actor will cause a fuss or take advantage.

My first inclination was to shoot close-ups of individual chicks with and without their parents in the hazy veil of blowing snow. Then I decided to move back with a telephoto lens and emphasize the white-out conditions that almost obscured a large group of chicks that were about to molt into adult plumage and looked nearly as big as their parents, who were mostly out to sea. Both parents will soon return full of shrimplike krill to regurgitate for these voracious adolescents, who can't forage in the sea until they molt. When the chicks were smaller, one parent was always present to foil air attacks by fierce skuas, polar predators that look like gulls but behave more like raptors. In a world without the foxes, wolves, or bears of the Arctic, penguins fear no ground attacks. *(Nikon F4, 80–200 f2.8 lens, f11 at 1 second, Fuji Velvia)*

Eskimo children in traditional winter furs beside the Arctic Ocean on Point Barrow, Alaska; 1994 *p. 18*

These children are walking the ice edge of the Arctic Ocean beyond the town of Barrow on a -30°F winter day. Their fur garments were made at home by their mother, Nora Rexford. She says that the value of the pelts plus the long hours she spends sewing them would price each set of garments at well over $2,000, if she made them for sale. Complete outfits such as these are now rarely worn except for special occasions, although traditional items are still in use for rugged winter travels, such as parkas with ruffs of wolf and wolverine fur or mukluks made out of caribou or polar bear fur. According to a U.S. military handbook on survival, an Eskimo caribou suit provides better insulation pound for pound than any combination of synthetic high-tech gear made especially for cold weather.

I composed the image with lots of open, untracked snow in front of the children to show their environment and impart a stronger sense of motion than a more centered composition would convey. The camera was handheld with a manual exposure reading set from the blue sky. A remote battery pack in my shirt pocket next to my warm body kept the electronics working via a cord running to a dummy plug in the camera. *(Nikon N90, 24mm f2.8 lens, f8 at 1/250 second, Fuji Velvia)*

Emperor penguins and visitor, Weddell Sea, Antarctica; 1993 *p. 19*

During the first tourist visit to recently discovered emperor penguin colonies along the remote Riiser-Larsen Ice Shelf of the Weddell Sea, Richard Hirsch dressed in kind. The tuxedo and the idea of trying to mime the Chaplinesque movements of these three-and-a-half-foot-tall flightless birds were his own. An attorney who worked his way through college as a clown, Richard was the self-appointed spokesman for our species to meet the locals on their own terms.

This photograph was made in a different colony on a far better day than the one on page 17. The spring temperature on a good summer day in December was only a few degrees below freezing, so I was able to handle cameras with ease and manually hold focus on the foreground penguins as they moved slowly away from the weird creature they had just come to check out. They seemed less concerned about me, possibly because I stopped and let them approach me, while Richard appeared as a strange apparition on the move. The penguins soon veered off their path to join a nearby group engaged in the new sport of people-watching.

The clean whites and rich blacks were achieved by using a manual exposure off my palm—about one stop open from a direct reading off the ice, which would have rendered the scene dark gray. With the camera on a tripod well back from the scene, I was able to use a telephoto effect to compress the distance between the penguins and the human figure. *(Nikon N90, 80–200mm f2.8 lens, f8 at 1/125 second, Fuji Velvia)*

Late August sea ice at the geographic North Pole, Arctic Ocean; 1993 *p. 22*

Making an interpretive landscape photograph right at the North Pole was something I never would have done without conscious forethought. I previsualized possible images and wrote down ideas well before we arrived on a Russian nuclear icebreaker. Distractions were myriad, from a champagne toast on the bridge to a barbecue on the pack ice, a Russian riding his motorscooter around the pole, female crew members posed on an ice floe in tight skirts and fur coats, group photos at the bow, and even a polar plunge through a hole in the ice into exposed seawater at the stern (for which I warmed up by running around the ship in shorts through all the world's time zones).

We were favored by an absolutely still day, with temperatures that rose above freezing to 34°F when the sun came out just after we arrived (unlike the -45°F I had found at the South Pole at 9,300 feet). The downside of the warmth was the lack of sharply etched ice features except on the shadowed side of a raised block of pack ice kicked up by a pressure ridge. It would not have made a decent straight photograph in deep shadow, but by using fill flash at close range with a wide-angle lens, I was able to balance a richly exposed dark sky with just enough light on the foreground icicles. I used a warming gel over the flash to match the pinkish color around a sun that was quite low on the horizon. On August 31, we were only twenty-two days from the beginning of complete winter darkness that would last for six months. *(Nikon F4, 24mm f2.8 lens, SB-25 flash, f8 at 1/250 second, Fuji Velvia)*

Dome of the United States Amundsen-Scott South Pole Station; 1992 *p. 23*

To give the South Pole something of the same spherical feeling as when we look at it on a globe or a satellite photograph, I used an extremely wide-angle 16mm lens that curves horizons placed off-center in the frame. With my camera on a small tripod, I lay on the edge of the roof of the adjoining four-story Skylab and peered down and over the 165-foot metal dome that covers some of the other buildings at the South Pole Station to keep them from drifting in with snow and getting buried in ice. Beneath the roof of the dome are two-story buildings for living, dining, communications, meetings, lab work, and recreation, plus a garage complex, gym, carpentry shop, and biomedical facility. Fuel bladders hold 225,000 gallons of diesel fuel to run the station during the nine months of the year when it is wholly isolated and populated only by a skeleton crew of about twenty winter-over personnel. Summer populations can exceed 125.

The station was built 400 yards from the surveyed position of the pole in 1975, but as the glacial ice moves, at a rate of about 10 yards a year, it gradually approaches the true pole. A previous polar station built in 1957 slowly began to drift over and was abandoned when this one was completed in 1975. The floor of the old station is now almost a hundred feet below the surface. Most of the accumulation is due to the wind, not the 2 inches of annual precipitation that fall on this polar desert. Nothing melts here where the temperature averages -57°F. *(Nikon F4, 16mm f2.8 lens, f8 at 1/125 second, Fuji Velvia)*

Summer in the Cirque of the Unclimbables, Northwest Territories, Canada; 1993 *p. 26*

My first visits to this paradise of alpine meadows and granite walls with poetic names like Lotus Flower Tower were in 1972 and 1973. When I finally returned twenty years later with two friends to climb a face on Mount Proboscis that drops into an adjoining valley, I had a burning desire to return to the main cirque and photograph it again. The images I had previously made really pleased me, and I wondered how much better I could do with more advanced knowledge and equipment. One day while my partners spent 15 hours working out free-climbing moves on 15 feet of rock, I opted to solo across the steep ridge separating the valleys. I knew that a top climber of the sixties had taken a bad fall on the route, so I kept my camera gear to a minimum with a body and two lenses plus a 1.5-pound tripod. To my pleasant surprise, I found a reasonable way down the almost vertical, moss-covered granite into a valley I had entirely to myself. I wandered around for hours under threatening skies, realizing that I actually liked the cloudy light better than direct sun.

To get this scene with Stonehenge-like foreground rocks playing off 2,000-foot granite spires in the distance, I needed to set up a tripod at least 6 feet above the ground. My tiny one didn't go above waist level, so I put my camera on it and held it against another rock with sideways pressure. *(Nikon 8008s, 24mm f2.8 lens, f11 at 1/15 second, Fuji Velvia)*

Summer in the Lemaire Channel, Antarctic Peninsula; 1991 *p. 27*

I made this image from the bow of the *Professor Molchanov*, a scientific research vessel from the Soviet Arctic that had been chartered just before the breakup of the Soviet Union to carry tourists to Antarctica. Despite the wildly Antarctic appearance of this scene, our voyage never crossed the Antarctic Circle. Although much of our cruise was in rough water, as we cruised through the narrow Lemaire Channel, both water and air were absolutely still. Icebergs floated silently beneath tidewater glaciers, from which they had broken off. Even in these ideal conditions, shooting photographs from a moving boat is much the same as aerial photography. Fast shutter speeds, wide-open apertures, and scenes entirely at infinity without close foregrounds are the order of the day. I put a very fast 35mm *f1*.4 moderately wide-angle lens on my camera with film pushed one stop for both extra speed and contrast in the flat light. A special Singh-Ray two-stop soft-edged graduated neutral-density filter held detail in the sky with an open exposure for the darker foreground. *(Nikon F4, 35mm f1.4 lens, f1.4 at 1/500 second, Fuji Velvia push processed to ISO 100)*

Arctic winter obscures the edge of a continent near Barrow, Alaska; 1994 *p. 30*

While flying back from a native village, Barrow pilot Jerry Jordan asked me if there was anything special I wanted to photograph. We had searched the ice edge for wildlife and found none. Dramatic contours were absent, because the coastline was so blanketed with ice and snow. Suddenly I realized that was it: the picture was what I *didn't see* where continent and ocean meet. The surf, the motion, the cliffs, the abrupt change in color, and the teeming life that we so take for granted along temperate coastlines were simply not there. After not seeing anything to photograph a minute before, I now had an exciting new vision of the sameness of the ocean and the land as a hallmark of Arctic winter. Knowing that I had a complementary photo from the Weddell Sea in the South, I imagined a continuation of the ice edge in that image and asked Jerry to circle higher and farther out from the coast, where I could better emphasize the apparent insignificance of this winter coast. Even on the ground in this frozen world, you are never certain which step takes you from land to sea or back again. *(Nikon N90, 35mm f1.4 lens, f1.4 at 1/2000 second, Fuji Velvia push processed to ISO 100)*

New ice forming in the Weddell Sea off the Riiser-Larsen Ice Shelf, Antarctica; 1993 *p. 31*

After we crossed the Antarctic Circle and headed deep into the Weddell Sea on the Russian icebreaker *Kapitan Khlebnikov*, we abruptly entered the pack ice beside a trapped iceberg over 100 feet high. The new ice beside the open sea was so thin and salty that it undulated with the waves. In the distance, the Riiser-Larsen Ice Shelf floats imperceptibly as if it were solid land. Larger than many states of the Union, the ice shelf on top of the sea is anchored fast to continental land a full 100 miles away, far out of the range of my camera.

In this pairing of images, the false coastline of the Far South appears more prominent than the real coast of the Far North, which is hidden by ice and snow. I used a fast lens so I could handhold my camera at a high shutter speed from the bridge of the ship to stop the motion as we bore down on the ice pack. *(Nikon N90, 35mm f1.4 lens, f1.4 at 1/1000 second, Fuji Velvia)*

Birch and spruce near Arctic treeline, Brooks Range, Alaska; 1993 *p. 32*

I selected this small group of trees as representative of the edge of the Arctic while driving back to Fairbanks from Prudhoe Bay over the gravel road beside the Alaska Pipeline. Although the state legislature christened the route the "Dalton Highway," nobody calls it that. Despite its official closure to public use, the "Haul Road" has become an unkept-secret getaway for Alaskan hunters and outdoor enthusiasts in recent years. I have yet to hear of anyone being turned back. On my way to Prudhoe, I had kept right on going past these trees because I hoped to find a sharp boundary of forest and tundra precisely at the northernmost extent of treeline some miles up the road. Instead, the trees were in isolated clumps, much like this but far less attractive. Here the vegetation was concentrated beside raised ridges of dark earth that gave me a perfect, slightly elevated perspective with a 35mm lens on a tripod. Use of a two-stop graduated neutral-density filter held detail in the brighter landscape and sky in the distance. Afterward, I found out that the site I had chosen for its visual attributes at mile 163 had been extensively studied by scientists as a classic example of a peat island near the southern margin of the continuous permafrost zone. Radiocarbon dates confirmed that the peat and the tree pollens within it were no older than 9,600 years, closely corresponding with the end of the last ice age of the Pleistocene. Here was a spot that straddled the edges of several common Arctic definitions. The northernmost treeline, the southernmost continuous permafrost, and the Arctic Circle were all within one degree of latitude of each other at this point. *(Nikon F4, 35mm f2 lens, f16 at 1/4 second, Fuji Velvia)*

Ventifact at Bull Pass, Dry Valleys, Transantarctic Mountains, Antarctica; 1992 *p. 33*

In the eerie Dry Valleys of Antarctica, which provide Earth's closest analog to the surface of Mars, rocks appear to have been sculpted by intelligent beings. Called ventifacts, these naturally created artifacts are the result of eons of sandblasting by wind-borne rock and ice. After spending a week camping in Taylor Valley with scientists, I had their Navy helicopter drop me at Bull Pass for a few hours while they ferried equipment and personnel from McMurdo Station. I wandered with my camera over an ancient erosion surface that may not have been disturbed by ice or strong geological action for 10 million years. I was captivated by the look of many of the smaller ventifacts that were worn into steep pyramids looking like peaks that had been carved by glaciers. Their most sculpted and polished facades all face toward the ice sheet of the Polar Plateau, the source of the fierce katabatic winds that blow almost every day of the year. Thus the ventifacts appear to be expressing a common gesture in the same direction, like the rocks of Stonehenge or Easter Island, that conveys a sense of purposeful design. This particular 10-foot block of relatively soft Beacon sandstone has undergone extreme cavernous weathering beyond the smoothing of its faces, which gives it the look of an incomplete Henry Moore sculpture. I used a wide-angle lens with a polarizing filter to emphasize my impression of stark contrast and open space. As Barry Lopez wrote after a visit to Bull Pass, "On the grasslands of the Serengeti, you can feel the vitality of the original creation; in the Dry Valleys you sense sharply what came before." *(Nikon N90, 24mm f2.8 lens, f16 at 1/30 second, Fuji Velvia)*

Moth on moss campion, Cirque of the Unclimbables, Northwest Territories, Canada; 1993 *p. 34*

On my first trip into the remote Cirque of the Unclimbables in the seventies, I had been fascinated by green mats of moss campion with pink flowers growing on the faces of the granite spires over 1,000 feet above the valley floor. Without a tripod on those climbs, none of my photographs came out well. When I returned to climb the face of Mount Proboscis (see page 118), I had several days to myself while my two companions, using fixed ropes, rehearsed the hardest moves before our successful first ascent of a route that involved the most continuously difficult free climbing of any mountain wall yet climbed. I brought a tiny 1.5-pound Gitzo tripod to use on the final ascent and decided to take it on a solo climb of a nearby spire. On top was a film can with a note left by the last climber—Royal Robbins had been there thirty years to the week before me and was going to climb Proboscis the next day. On the descent, I came across this patch of moss campion with a moth sucking nectar out of the flowers. I almost passed it by because I had envisioned a photograph of a whole plant attached to the rock, without the interruption of the insect. What made me decide to focus tightly on the moth was a bit of whimsy. I recalled that a moth obtains nectar from a flower through an extended tubular mouthpart called a proboscis. The sluggish moth never budged in the cool alpine air as I set up my macro lens on my tripod inches away and stopped down for maximum depth of field. *(Nikon 8008s, 55mm f2.8 lens, f32 at 1/2 second, Fuji Velvia)*

Antarctic pink and bundle grass, King George Island, South Shetland Islands, Antarctica; 1993 *p. 35*

During my ship's short stop at the Polish base of Arctowski at latitude 62° south, a scientist pointed me toward meager tufts of Antarctica's only two flowering plants growing in a sheltered spot just above tide line. The species, *Colobanthus quientensis* and *Deschampsia antarctica*, rarely grow together except where they receive fresh water from glacial melt, climate moderation at the edge of the sea facing the sun, and fertilization from a bird colony. I pondered how to make an interesting image of a subject I would otherwise ignore and found a way to include the orange lichens, which thrive around penguin droppings. On Sir James Clark Ross's famous 1839–1843 Antarctic voyage, Joseph Dalton Hooker, the young assistant surgeon of the *Erebus*, collected *Deschampsia* grass in Patagonia, but missed it in Antarctica. Only twenty-two when the journey began, he became the greatest international botanist of the century. Before the voyage, he met with another young scientist who had recently spent four years at sea: Charles Darwin. Afterward, Hooker became Darwin's closest confidant, supplying so much of the botanical basis for the theory of evolution that Darwin's son later wrote, "The history of my father's life is told more completely in his correspondence with Sir J. D. Hooker than in any other series of letters." Hooker collected 18 species of tiny cryptogamous Antarctic plants, such as algae, fungi, and mosses, on journeys that reached 79° south, missing the only two vascular plants, which are not found south of 69° south. In comparison, about 1,000 species of vascular plants grow north of the Arctic Circle at 66° north. *(Nikon F4, 55mm f2.8 lens, f32 at 1 second, Fuji Velvia)*

Breaking through fresh ice at 84° north in the Arctic Ocean; 1993 *p. 36*

As the Russian nuclear icebreaker *Yamal* plowed through an average of 6 feet of sea ice en route to the North Pole, we often encountered open water. Sometimes we crossed leads caused by stress cracks in the pack that would open and close with the currents. However, the largest stretches of open water were ice-locked pools called *polynyas*, which can be hundreds of feet or hundreds of miles across with discrete boundaries that stay more or less the same for months or years at a time. In mid-September the surface of these polynyas is often coated with young sea ice called *nilas*, which, unlike the brittle sheets on freshwater ice over lakes and ponds, forms highly elastic sheets because of its strong brine content. The wake of a ship can turn a seemingly hard surface of nilas into swells of dark ripples that glimmer without breaking. I once saw a polar bear cross 50 feet of nilas on its belly without going through.

In this kaleidoscopic scene off the ship's bow, plates of nilas several inches thick are rapidly "finger-rafting" on top of one another at the moment we reenter the pack ice. Thick blocks of blue-green ice churn at the lower right as plates of nilas begin to slide over the preexisting pattern caused by natural finger-rafting in high winds and heavy seas. To make this photograph from a ship moving at 20 knots, I used a very fast wide-angle lens with film pushed one stop to freeze the action in dim light with a high shutter speed. *(Nikon N90, 35mm f1.4 lens, f1.4 at 1/500 second, Fuji Velvia push processed to ISO 100)*

Phytoplankton bloom beneath 15 feet of sea ice, McMurdo Sound, Ross Sea, Antarctica; 1992 *p. 37*

I made this photograph with a standard camera at a remote camp where biologist Ward Testa was studying the behavior of Weddell seals. To monitor activity beneath the sea ice, his team used radio telemetry plus a narrow observation tube set into a drilled hole. When I dropped into the dim, murky world, my hopes of photographing seals beneath the ice were instantly dashed. I had read that phytoplanktons beneath the ice receive about 1 percent of the surface light. That translated to a 1/250 shutter speed with my 85mm *f*1.4 lens and ISO 200 film. Instead, my meter read 1 second, indicating a full 2,000 times less light than at the surface. The spring bloom had also reduced underwater visibility from a winter maximum of well over 100 feet to 20 feet. When I heard a seal bark, I saw nothing until it suddenly appeared, ghostlike, beneath the ice. As it nosed around for fish feeding off the bloom, I realized that a clear image of the sea ice from below could be more revealing than one of the seal. The rich green display of sea life is at the base of a food chain that moves upward through zooplankton (such as krill) to fish to birds and mammals more commonly seen by Antarctic visitors. The algae that form the phytoplankton blanket are actually yellowish, but the extreme blueness of the light passing through ice and water creates a green appearance from below. I used a long exposure with a wide-angle lens held firmly against the thick observation glass to capture more on slow film than I could see with my eyes. *(Nikon F4, 20mm f2.8 lens, f5.6 at 1/4 second, Fuji Velvia)*

Alaskan brown bear on its hind legs (captive), Chilkat Valley, Alaska; 1990 *p. 38*

The humanlike appearance of a standing bear triggers emotional responses that run the gamut from endearing in children's books, to fascinating on film, to totally frightening in a wild encounter. Among the large mammals of the Arctic, only the bear and the human walk with plantigrade feet, applying the whole sole to the ground as they move. Alaskan brown bear tracks up to 18 inches long give rise to many Bigfoot reports. Although I have photographed wild brown bears standing up, this image of a trained captive bear evokes a stronger response to its human demeanor. I took it on location for Walt Disney in Alaska while shooting promotional stills for the film *White Fang*. Where the script called for a grizzly attack, the chosen actor was Bart, a 1,400-pound subarctic Alaskan brown bear and a lead in the Hollywood feature *The Bear*. The film crew warned Barbara and me that trainer Doug Seus was more difficult to deal with than Bart, who had clobbered the director of *The Bear* as he unwisely tried to pose next to Bart without Doug around. Bart obeys Doug because Doug thinks and behaves like the dominant bear and, armed with nothing more than a sawed-off bat, has yet to back down from a challenge. Barbara and I also obeyed Doug, armed with nothing more than a camera or two. We became fast and lasting friends. After shooting a key scene, Doug had Bart strike a standing pose for me in front of an Alaskan peak that I feel symbolizes the wave of giantism followed by extinction that swept through Arctic mammals during the Pleistocene, leaving the brown bear as the world's largest land predator. *(Nikon F4, 80–200 f2.8 lens, f5.6 at 1/250 second, Fuji Velvia)*

Molting king penguin chick, Saint Andrews Bay, South Georgia Island, Subantarctic; 1993 (photograph by Barbara Cushman Rowell) *p. 39*

While I stood on a hill trying to compose a broad overview of half a million king penguins, Barbara moved in close to single out a juvenile in the process of molting into the tightly bunched adult feathers that will allow it to survive in the cold sea after nearly a year of total dependence on its parents. It just stood there, content not to move as it waited for a parent to return with food; meanwhile, Barbara got down on her knees about 8 feet away, with her tripod at its lowest position to get an eye-level view through a medium telephoto lens. She used an aperture of *f*5.6 to hold the bird sharp, but let the background blur. With no other size cues present, the eye-level perspective adds another facet to the human characteristics that endear penguins to us. Barbara selected this chick because it appeared to have a zany personality she could relate to. She imagined it as a scruffy masked marauder among a crowd of perfectly appointed ladies and gentlemen, sort of like Darth Vader trying to look inconspicuous at a cocktail party. I chose Barbara's image over thousands of my own penguin photos because it reveals more of the nature of these creatures that typify the Antarctic in the public mind. Caught between early life as a downy chick on land and adulthood as a true marine animal, this single bird is a visual metaphor for the strange evolutionary transition of its species. Soon it will be beating its modified wings to literally fly underwater at great speed, instead of merely paddling water with its feet, like flying birds who make only occasional dives. *(Nikon F4, 80–200mm f2.8 lens, f5.6 at 1/15 second, Fuji Velvia)*

Breaching gray whale, Bahía Magdalena, Baja California, Mexico; 1994 *p. 40*

The "California gray whale" is a sad misnomer for a splendid Arctic creature. Today, grays are most commonly seen migrating past the populous Pacific Coast, but until intensive whaling began, they were common residents of many seas in the Circumpolar North. They evolved from a land mammal that adapted to the annual ice pack of the Arctic by developing the longest mammalian migration routes on Earth. Early Dutch sailors suspected the existence of a Northeast Passage over the top of Asia to the Pacific because a whale, which may have been from the now-extinct Atlantic race of grays, arrived off Korea with a harpoon from the Norwegian Arctic. By 1800, whalers had decimated the Atlantic population. Today's surviving grays live in the Arctic Ocean near the Bering Strait and migrate southward along both Pacific coasts. The American population makes a 12,000-mile round-trip to lagoons in Baja, where calves conceived in the Arctic are born. During the twenty years after 1857, when whaling captain Charles Scammon followed a pod into the lagoon that bears his name, about half of the remaining population—10,000 gray whales—were slaughtered. By 1900, they neared extinction. Protective measures failed until coverage by the 1972 Marine Mammal Protection Act and the Endangered Species Act. They were delisted as endangered in 1994 after numbers grew to over 20,000. With a handheld telephoto I caught this breach as Barbara and I walked down a beach where we had been camping for a week after she had flown our Cessna T206 over the major lagoons. I chose this shot over aerials showing groups of whales and calves near the surface because of this breach's amazing similarity to the breach of another marine-adapted creature from the opposite pole. *(Nikon N90, 400mm f5.6 ED lens, f5.6 at 1/500 second, Fuji Velvia)*

Emperor penguin breaching onto the ice edge, Riiser-Larsen colony, Weddell Sea, Antarctica; 1993 *p. 41*

Like the gray whale on the facing page, the emperor is a marine animal that adapted to life in the sea from an entirely different realm. Now flightless and clumsy on land, they seem as agile as porpoises in the sea. During the first tourist voyage into the Weddell Sea, the captain of our Russian icebreaker rammed his 800-ton vessel into the pack ice so that we could walk a mile to visit an emperor colony (see page 17). When we returned to the ship, I noticed that some emperors who had been out to sea were hanging around in the quiet waters of the miniature bay formed in the wake of our ship. Soon they began to zip around the pool, gather speed, and breach like torpedoes out of the water onto the ice edge. I lay down behind the lip and shot two 36-exposure rolls of film with a telephoto lens set at 1/2000 second. I was excited by what I saw through my viewfinder, but uncertain if anything would come out. When I had the film processed, this frame jumped out at me, far exceeding any other. All my autofocus shots of the fast-moving birds were fuzzy. Birds were rarely in the right place on frames where I had just let the motor drive rip as the birds broke the surface. This frame was the result of prefocusing on a spot and many attempts at timing the split-second interval from the first sound of breaking water. *(Nikon F4, 85mm f2 lens, f2.8 at 1/2000 second, Fuji Velvia push processed to ISO 100)*

Polar bear diving into the Arctic Ocean off Franz Josef Land, Russian Arctic; 1993 *p. 42*

Before traveling to the North Pole on a Russian nuclear icebreaker, I saw tight close-ups of polar bears taken on the first tourist journey in 1991. I never got such a shot myself, because the Russian crew of the brand-new *Yamal* had almost no experience with tourism. Each time we saw a bear, the crew chased the poor animal instead of easing alongside and letting its natural curiosity take over about a 22,000-ton intruder entering the realm it had always dominated. After eliciting a solemn promise that the ship would stop for the next bear, I stationed myself on the bow with a long telephoto lens propped on a beanbag as we approached a bold animal standing its ground on the ice. Yet again the ship plowed ahead, but I was ready to make the best of the situation. As the bow came close to striking the bear before it dove, I kept the animal in focus using the instant manual override on a Nikon 300mm *f*2.8 AFI autofocus lens with a 2x teleconverter for a total of 600mm. I composed the bear in the lower corner to keep the bow out of the frame and held focus on its backside as it plunged into the ocean—a visual metaphor for the evolution of a land predator into a marine mammal that can survive entirely off the sea. Weeks earlier, I had been lucky to photograph the only polar bear in years to come ashore at Prudhoe Bay in summer. Although it had swum a hundred miles from the nearest pack ice, my best close-ups at water's edge fail to tell the story communicated by this moment of departure. *(Nikon N90, 300mm f2.8 AFI lens with 2x teleconverter, f5.6 at 1/250, Fuji Velvia push processed to ISO 100)*

Mummy seal in Taylor Valley, Dry Valleys, Transantarctic Mountains, Antarctica; 1992 *p. 43*

Even though I had seen photographs of the mummy seals of the Dry Valleys, actually finding one during a 20-mile walk through a lifeless moonscape was a bizarre experience. On a -15°F spring morning with a 20 mph wind, I headed out in running shoes with chemical toe warmers, telling myself that I would turn around if my feet began to lose feeling. When I first saw the seal, the texture of its fur seemed alive. For a split second, I thought dog. In the next instant, the twisted body and grotesque grin clearly communicated death, yet without the slightest scent or hint of organic decay. The erosion looked as entirely geological as that of surrounding rocks ground smooth by windblown particles. After I spent long minutes composing a photo with a Singh-Ray two-stop graduated neutral-density to subdue the sunlit background, I noticed that my toes and fingers had gone numb. I wondered how long the young seal had survived here, less than 20 miles from the sea, and whether disorientation—the best guess of scientists—was the true cause of its final journey. Perhaps the seal felt as comfortable as I did before stopping, reasonably secure about retracing a route to safety if things did not go well. I suspect that even if disorientation plays a role, the gene pool of every animal population breeds a few wanderers who once in a while discover unoccupied niches that lead to the evolution of new species, such as the whale, the polar bear, and, not inconceivably, the walking land seal that may yet evolve as the climate of Antarctica warms. *(Nikon N90, 24mm f2.8 lens, f16 at 1/8 second, Fuji Velvia)*

Polar bear mother with cubs-of-the-year beside Hudson Bay near Churchill, Manitoba, Canada; 1993 *p. 44*

During the ice ages of the late Pleistocene, when outsized land mammals roamed the Arctic, the ancestors of the polar bear began to exploit a previously unoccupied predatory niche apart from the formidable world of mammoths, saber-toothed tigers, and giant short-faced bears. Scientists now believe that a brief moment ago, geologically speaking, an ancestral brown bear we would instantly recognize as a "grizzly" discovered easy pickings among the Arctic seals living on the sea ice. Polar bears began to evolve a separate lineage from those brown bears that occasionally took to the water to fish or scavenge about 200,000 years ago. The new bear rapidly became a marine mammal with an insulating layer of seal-like blubber, a longer neck, shorter ears, bigger and partially webbed feet, black skin, and colorless hair for perfect ice camouflage. It no longer had a dietary mandate for winter hibernation. Zoologists long considered the species to be in a genus of its own until new evidence forced them to place it in the genus *Ursus* with Arctic land bears, despite the unique attributes that allow it to survive on the ice or in the sea entirely apart from land. The genes of polar bears are so close to those of Alaskan brown bears that the two creatures have bred fertile offspring in captivity, breaching the strict definition of a separate species. To photograph this mother quietly guarding her cubs in a snowstorm, I used a 500mm lens plus 1.4x teleconverter for a total of 720mm on a 12-pound Gitzo tripod set up inside Donnie Wolkowski's tundra-tired "Photo Pro" vehicle. *(Nikon F4, 500mm f4 lens with 1.4x teleconverter, f5.6 at 1/60 second, Fuji Velvia push processed to ISO 100)*

Weddell seal and pup minutes after birth, McMurdo Sound, Antarctica; 1992 *p. 45*

A Weddell seal mother calmly giving birth on the open ice provides a clue to life in the Pleistocene for Arctic seals before the polar bear evolved. I had observed this pregnant seal lying motionless as I photographed around Ward Testa's Weddell seal study area on sea ice beneath Mount Erebus. She gave no hint of impending birth until she suddenly raised her tail. I happened to glimpse the placenta emerging before she partly lowered her tail, squirmed for a minute, and deposited a dark bundle almost hidden from view in a pool of red on the ice. I took this photograph a few minutes later with a long telephoto on a tripod so as not to disturb the scene as the baby slowly began to orbit its mother. It held a raised flipper firmly against her warm body as it tentatively explored a new environment 120°F colder than the cozy, windless womb it had just left, perhaps seeking a way back in. Weddell pups are extremely vulnerable to the elements and suffer a high first-year mortality rate. Testa's researchers were investigating factors influencing the survival of juvenile seals, but none had witnessed an actual birth except Testa himself, who had seen two in thirteen years. What adult Weddell seals fear most is the freezing of the ice hole that is their lifeline to breathing from below or getting food from above. With teeth modified for perpetual ice cutting to maintain open holes, Weddells are nearly impossible to keep in captivity: they instinctively gnaw their teeth and jaws away on concrete or any other substance used to contain them, until they die. *(Nikon F4, 500mm f4 lens with 2X teleconverter, f5.6 at 1/60 second, Fuji Velvia push processed to ISO 100)*

Pacific walrus, Arakamchechen Island, Chukchi Peninsula, Siberia; 1993 *p. 46*

The Arakamchechen Nature Preserve was created to protect the last large walrus colony off the tip of Siberia, but when I arrived in 1993, the population had dropped to 3,000 from 15,000 in 1991. Severe poaching in the wake of Russia's economic hardships and government wild-meat quotas to feed native arctic fox farms were the main causes. The only permitted vantage point for the shy animals was a roped-off ridgetop far above their haul-out beach. The warden insisted that my group spend only a few minutes, so as not to disturb the animals. Realizing that this might be my best Siberian walrus opportunity, even though it seemed mediocre, I tried to think of every possible way to hedge my bet and get a tight, sharp image of wet animals glowing pink fresh out of the sea. I braced a 300mm lens with a 2x teleconverter on a rock, while supporting the camera on a tripod, but ended up with too slow a shutter speed to stop the motion of moving walrus heads. To rescue the seemingly hopeless situation I pushed Fuji Velvia two stops to increase the shutter speed to 1/250 second and at the same time add a normally unwanted gain in contrast and warmth to cut through the flat, hazy, blue shadows. As I lay waiting to freeze the right moment, the quiet animals suddenly lifted their heads in alarm. It wasn't my group that had disturbed them, but the wildly gesticulating Russian warden who was standing at the edge of the cliff motioning for us to leave. I kept my eye to the viewfinder and went right on shooting until, seconds later, the walrus were in the sea. *(Nikon F4, 300mm f2.8 lens with 2X teleconverter, f4 at 1/250 second, Fuji Velvia push processed to ISO 200)*

Southern elephant seal, Grytviken, South Georgia Island, Subantarctic; 1993 *p. 47*

I chose this image over a previous frame that included a small human figure standing with a camera beside this immense bull, close to 20 feet long. The other frame drew too much attention to the alarmed human to pair with an image of wild walrus. Moments earlier, the bull had been resting with a glazed look in its open eyes. As the European tourist stepped close with a point-and-shoot camera, the animal sprang up with a sonic roar. As in a scene out of *King Kong*, bystanders fled in terror. Having anticipated the action, I was set up with a telephoto lens on a tripod to keep shooting as the tourist fled. Within seconds, the bull dropped its head as if nothing had happened. Bulls are so oblivious to everything on land except other bulls to spar with or females to mate with that they wallow through penguin colonies like living bulldozers, crushing eggs and chicks in their wake, and often kill pups of their own species by accidentally rolling over on them during territorial battles. Yet water transforms them into graceful divers that can stay under for two hours and reach depths of over 2,000 feet. Because they lack substantial fur, they were not hunted until the mid-1800s, after Antarctic fur seals had become scarce and whales were declining. Then elephant seals by the hundreds of thousands were rendered into oil until they, too, were almost gone by the turn of the century. Commercial hunts stopped, except on South Georgia where the British figured out a way to harvest up to 6,000 a year with almost no decline in population. Until shore-based whaling and sealing ceased in 1965, only bulls that were reproductively irrelevant were killed, leaving the dominant beachmasters to mate with their harems. Southern elephant seal numbers have now recovered to over 700,000. *(Nikon N90, 80–200 f2.8 lens, f4 at 1/125 second, Fuji Velvia)*

Reindeer herd on the Chukchi Peninsula, Siberia; 1993 *p. 48*

The reindeer of Eurasia and the caribou of North America belong to the same species, *Rangifer tarandus.* They appear so similar that individuals cannot be positively identified apart from their herd. Reindeer are slightly paler, shorter, and more placid, although this group herded by Chukchi natives on the eastern tip of Siberia happens to be quite dark. Six vague subspecies are defined by biologists, but what separates the two creatures far more decisively is their past and present relationship to Arctic peoples. Reindeer are domestic animals controlled by herdsmen whose lives have revolved around breeding and pasturing them since prehistoric times, except in remote parts of the Asian Arctic where a few wild, feral, or partly feral herds roam. About 15,000 Chukchi herders live in eastern Siberia with their animals, as do other native herders farther west across Arctic Asia and Europe. On the other side of the Bering Strait in Alaska and Canada, *Rangifer tarandus* has always been the wild caribou, except for a few modern herds of European reindeer imported for farming. The caribou owes its wildness to the sacred relationship the Eskimos of North America have with the natural world. They do not consider themselves separate from nature, as do most Anglo-Europeans. To take the wild character of life away from a creature is contrary to their worldview, although to take a life in order to feed or defend one's family is accepted, so long as it is done with proper respect. As Barry Lopez has written, "The great task of life for the traditional Eskimo is to achieve congruence with a reality that is already given." Thus caribou are to remain forever wild, and sled dogs are never allowed to be pets or to come inside the home. *(Nikon N90, 80–200mm f2.8 lens, f5.6 at 1/125 second, Fuji Velvia)*

Feral reindeer in king penguin colony, Saint Andrews Bay, South Georgia Island, Subantarctic; 1993 *p. 49*

To be observing Antarctic penguins and seals on South Georgia Island and see a herd of reindeer crest a ridge is good reason to question your sanity—unless you have learned something of the island's cultural history as well as its natural history. In 1904, the Norwegians established the permanent whaling settlement of Grytviken. The enterprise was so "successful" that 175,000 whales were taken in the first thirteen years. During that period, reindeer were introduced to raise for meat. Although the island's vegetation is biologically different from and far more sparse than the typical Arctic tundra favored by reindeer, spotty fell fields and patches of tussock grass allowed them to thrive with almost no competition from other mammals except the ubiquitous Norway rat and some introduced sheep and horses that did not survive. From the beginning, the reindeer ran free in the absence of full-time herders, within an area naturally hemmed in by glaciers. The Norwegians kept track of their limited movements and hunted them for sport and meat until in 1965 they abandoned both Grytviken and the reindeer. Since then, the overall global warming trend has melted back the glaciers enough to allow the reindeer to greatly expand their range. They now number over 2,000. I spotted this herd and stalked it with a 300mm lens on a tripod just after we landed the first Zodiac raft from our ship. The reindeer were so much more skittish than their Siberian counterparts that I suspected some hunting or culling must be going on without public notice. *(Nikon F4, 300mm f2.8 AFI lens, f2.8 at 1/500 second, Fuji Velvia)*

Horned puffin, Pribilof Islands, Bering Sea, Alaska; 1979 *p. 50*

When I photographed this puffin high on a sea cliff in the late seventies, I found it much harder to approach than puffins in less remote areas farther south. I later learned that the local Aleuts were stalking these puffins for food at the same time as they were promoting expensive birdwatching tours. I had to use hours of stealth and a 600mm lens braced in a crevice to get a decent portrait of a single puffin. I composed it against a cliff to hold it apart from the distraction of thousands of kittiwakes, murres, and auklets on the same cliff. The visual pairing of a puffin and a penguin works because of their convergent evolution. Their roughly parallel appearance coevolved poles apart on remote islands in cold seas. Their behavior, however, radically diverges. The puffin flies over open oceans and occasionally dives, while the penguin is flightless and as at home in the water as a seal. The greatest difference is in conspecific behavior toward members of their own species. Macaroni penguins can be snippy at times, but have a calm disposition compared with the horned puffin. "The only bird on these islands which seems to quarrel for ever and ever with its mate," a Mr. H. W. Elliot wrote in a report on the wildlife of the Pribilofs not long after the purchase of Alaska from Russia in 1867. "The hollow reverberations of its anger, scolding and vituperation from the nuptial chambers, are the most characteristic sounds, and indeed the only ones that come from the recesses of the rocks. No sympathy need be expended on the female. She is just as big and just as violent." *(Nikon FM, 600mm f8 Novoflex lens, f8 at 1/60 second, Kodachrome 64)*

Macaroni penguin, Saunders Island, South Sandwich Islands, Subantarctic; 1993 *p. 51*

The happy-go-lucky look of the red-eyed, orange-plumed macaroni penguin is in stark contrast to its habitat on the South Sandwich Islands—"the most dreary starved appearance that can be imagined," as described in the log of Captain James Cook's ship when he discovered the islands in 1775. Although both the islands and the macaroni penguins are generally called subantarctic, geographers classify the South Sandwich group, which is surrounded by pack ice every winter, as true "Antarctic maritime islands." Thus the habitat of the birds here and at the few rare spots where they breed on the Antarctic Peninsula and on nearby islands is distinct from the subantarctic, where a far larger breeding population of about 24 million macaronis flourishes around the lush tussock grasses of South Georgia Island. When early British explorers encountered these conspicuous dandies of the penguin world amidst their more sedately attired black-and-white neighbors, they were reminded of the orange-plumed caps worn by gentlemen who belonged to the Macaroni Club of London. I discovered their resemblance to the horned puffins of the Arctic while sorting slides on my light box for this book just after returning from the Antarctic. Without my reading glasses on, I momentarily thought I saw a macaroni penguin, with its clear white underparts, full black collar, and spots of orange and red on its head, among a set of Arctic bird slides at the edge of the box. I realized that these very disparate birds from opposite polar regions, as well as from different species, families, and orders, had coevolved a remarkably similar appearance, like that of a Tasmanian marsupial wolf and a mammalian wolf, by roughly parallel adaptations to life in specialized niches on islands in cold seas. *(Nikon N90, 80–200mm f2.8 lens, f4 at 1/125 second, Fuji Velvia push processed to ISO 100)*

Thick-billed murres nesting on sea cliffs on the Pribilof Islands, Bering Sea, Alaska; 1979 *p. 52*

Many biologists consider the tiny Pribilof Islands, surrounded by "the richest plankton soup north of the Galápagos" in the heart of the Bering Sea, to have the world's greatest concentration of mammals and seabirds. Unlike the Galápagos, these perpetually cold, windy, and damp islands have a distinctly Arctic climate. The 50°F summer isotherm that defines the Arctic life zone dips far south into the Bering Sea to encircle them. Thick-billed murres are the most common of the millions of flying birds from over 190 species that visit the rugged sea cliffs around the islands. They are members of the auk family, an Arctic counterpart to the penguins of the south. In fact, *penguin* was originally a name for the extinct 3.5-foot great auk; an early British sailor mistakenly used the same word to describe the strange flightless birds of the south. I photographed these four murres nesting in a row on the brink of a cliff while leading the first "Alaskan Wildlife Safari" for an adventure travel company in the late seventies. The trips were canceled within a couple of years because of mixed reviews and the logistical nightmare of following a tight, fixed schedule with frequent flights beset by unpredictable weather delays. Reaching the Pribilofs near the end of the trip after a long flight with stops in the Aleutians was like arriving in Mecca for the birders in our group, but so dismal for others that the mother of one family commented, "They ought to put a penal colony here." While part of the group stayed in town, several of us braved a stormy morning to sit atop the cliffs for hours, gain the birds' confidence, and photograph them with long lenses, biding our time until they appeared unconcerned about our presence. *(Nikon FM, 600mm f8 Novoflex lens, f8 at 1/60 second, Kodachrome 64)*

149

Adélie penguins at Cape Crozier, Ross Island, Antarctica; 1992 *p. 53*

Every spring, over 2 million Adélies hop out of the sea and waddle across the ice toward rare patches of windswept open ground. No other truly Antarctic penguin breeds on land. The Adélie and the emperor are the only ones that live and breed close to the continent within the zone of pack ice, and since emperor colonies are on sea ice, the annual treks of the Adélies are the closest Antarctic counterpart to the Arctic caribou migrations. I made this photograph while retracing the route of the 1911 "worst journey in the world" (see pages 92–93) to observe the Cape Crozier emperor penguin colony with biologist Gerald Kooyman and his team of researchers. As we descended the final snow slope within sight of the vast Ross Ice Shelf, distant, melodious chants of the emperors were broken by a raucous braying that sounded like a lost donkey. We could see a line of Adélies approaching a mile-wide swath of windblown hillside just above the sea ice. Upon arrival, they spread out toward previous nest sites, like the first sports fans finding reserved seats in an open-air coliseum. Kooyman told me that these were all males and that within two weeks the entire slope would be a solid carpet of breeding pairs. I used a telephoto lens to single out two Adélies involved in an "ecstatic display," which spreads outward from one individual like a cough in a theater. As the male nearest the camera arched its neck, pointed its head skyward, and flapped its flightless wings, the one behind followed suit. Strong black-and-white communication that has been likened to semaphores carries over into the sea, where the black-above, white-below pattern allows flocks to choreograph movements when side by side, yet camouflages them from leopard seals above or below. *(Nikon N90, 80–200mm f2.8 lens, f11 at 1/60 second, Fuji Velvia)*

Immature ivory gull, Hayes Island, Franz Josef Land, Russian Arctic; 1993 *p. 54*

The ivory gull's elusive reputation has as much to do with human behavior as with the low population of the species. The birds are seldom seen because they breed in the remote high Arctic and because their entirely white plumage is invisible against the snowy landscape, the pack ice, or the typically cloudy Arctic skies. Even when they appear out of nowhere, sophisticated autofocus cameras can't detect a contrast edge. I sought out immature birds with dark heads and wing edges to allow my Nikon 300mm autofocus lens to track them in midair. But first I had to find them. Earlier in the summer, I had caught only distant glimpses on extensive travels that took me by land across the Alaskan Brooks Range to the Arctic Ocean and by sea to the North Pole across the entire Northeast Passage and back by way of Greenland through eighteen time zones. When I arrived in Franz Josef Land by helicopter from an icebreaker, I happened on an Arctic birder's counterpart to the McNeil River convocation of brown bears fishing for salmon. As I walked up a hill onto the grounds of the Russian research station called Krenkel Observatory, dozens of ivory gulls were on the ground and circling in the air around a raised snow hill—the station's open garbage dump. Our ship's ornithologist, Arnold Small, who had a staggering life list of over 6,800 birds, had never seen or heard of anything like it. We both shot rolls of photographs of fearless ivory gulls landing and making passes within 20 feet of us. Although I got sharp images of adults in flight with manual focus, I chose this autofocus image of an immature bird because it perfectly anticipates the glide and stronger black-and-white plumage of the petrel on the opposite page. *(Nikon N90, 300mm f2.8 lens, f2.8 at 1/1000 second, Fuji Velvia push processed to ISO 100)*

Pintado petrel in a blizzard, Antarctic Sound, Antarctica; 1993 *p. 55*

A distant relative of the albatross, the pintado petrel is also a great flier that ranges entirely around Antarctica and two-thirds of the way northward toward the Equator. They glide over the sea for long minutes without flapping their wings, in synchronous flocks that remain almost invisible until they bank and fleetingly display the vivid black-and-white contrast of their plumage. Their flying behavior helps explain why this form of camouflage is in fact far more subtle than that of the white snow petrel of the Antarctic or the ivory gull of the Arctic. As biologist David Campbell so eloquently puts it, "Their backs are the color of sea foam on dark water; their bellies are pale as the sky. This is their camouflage. Each bears an inverted sea, sky, and horizon on its body in a realm that is only sea, sky, and horizon."

I once visited a pintado petrel breeding colony high on the cliffs of Deception Island. I could stand a few feet from birds taking off with hardly a flap of their wings into especially strong winds that accelerate through a gap. Many of my photographs were sharp and well exposed, but they failed to capture the special quality, so characteristic of the species, that comes through in this image of a bird just above the water in a snowstorm. The petrel was following the *Kapitan Khlebnikov* as we cruised through the Antarctic Sound on our way to the Weddell Sea. As it flew loops around the ship, I stood on the upper deck and used the "focus tracking" feature of my handheld Nikon N90 camera to firmly lock autofocus on the bird's contrasty plumage. *(Nikon N90, 80–200mm f2.8 lens, f2.8 at 1/500 second, Kodak Lumiere 100)*

Raven wing prints at 16,000 feet on Mount McKinley, Alaska; 1979 *p. 56*

I came across an expedition's food cache being ripped apart by ravens while traversing Mount McKinley with another team. We were carrying huge packs with everything we needed to survive for weeks in extreme Arctic conditions. (Later, we were indeed pinned down by a storm in temperatures that dropped to -35°F and winds that tore apart a tent.) Members of the other group were clearly planning on retracing their route. They were climbing toward the summit with lighter packs than ours, counting on their food cache for their return. Ravens had raided open food around camps on McKinley for years, but only in the late seventies did they discover that sealed bags usually had food inside and could be torn open with ease. We tried to scare the birds away from the cache, but they didn't move until we came close, waving our arms and yelling. Finally, all but one flew off. The bird that stayed back hesitated until we could almost grab it and attempted a takeoff that almost failed. It ran downhill, flapping its wings wildly, and used up most of the available runway before finally getting aloft. It was clearly over gross weight for takeoff at such an altitude. I quickly got out my camera and wide-angle lens to frame the line of wing prints into a vanishing diagonal before anyone else tracked up the virgin snow. The raven's difficulty getting airborne at high altitude is a clue to why much larger and heavier flying birds, comparable to the albatross, never evolved in the Arctic. The winds are not consistently strong enough to allow such a bird to land and take off. *(Nikon FM, 24mm f2.8 lens, f11 at 1/15 second, Kodachrome 64)*

Wandering albatross, Bay of Isles, South Georgia Island, Subantarctic; 1993 *p. 57*

On a perfect day with only a light breeze, I caught the world's largest flying bird hesitating before taking off from a high perch on its island breeding colony. Minutes later, another albatross attempted a takeoff from an even higher perch and failed. After it crash-landed in the grass, it was so exhausted by the effort of rapidly beating its wings that it just sat down for the better part of an hour before slowly trudging back up the steep hill. When the wind picked up later in the day, the same bird tried again and made it.

Until recently, wandering albatrosses had a life span of around fifty years. Biologists now note a worldwide decline in population of approximately 1 percent per year that is more related to the age of adult birds than to breeding success. The birds could become endangered within the next half century. The reasons are not fully understood, but competition for food with fishermen, entrapment in fishing nets, and addiction to the garbage thrown off boats are high on the list of suspected causes. Birds that have become habituated to fishing boats as food sources also tend to follow Antarctic cruise ships, providing tourists with their most frequent observations. These creatures with the longest wings of any living bird relish flying in stormy weather. The power of the wind allows them to glide for hours without flapping their wings through steep turns and swoops that touch the crests of waves. Without predators around their breeding colonies, wandering albatrosses are remarkably approachable. I spent hours within 10 or 15 feet of unconcerned birds involved in courtship displays or simply waiting for the wind to pick up so they could take off. I made this photograph with my camera on a tripod after waiting patiently until the bird stood and stretched its wings. *(Nikon F4, 80–200mm f2.8 lens, f5.6 at 1/250 second, Fuji Velvia)*

Arctic fox, Churchill, Manitoba, Canada; 1993 *p. 58*

Among the wild members of the dog family, only the arctic fox makes a complete visual adaptation to a polar environment. In summer, arctic foxes are brown or bluish gray. By November, foxes the color of winter have become virtually invisible unless they move. I have spotted a white fox running more than half a mile away in a snowstorm, only to fail to see one 20 feet away until it darted off. This fox is bursting away from a polar bear that took a swipe at it after it had ventured too close. Earlier that day, an experienced European wildlife photographer who had spent two seasons at Churchill told me it wouldn't be worth going out for photos during a blizzard. I froze the fox against the blowing snow with a high shutter speed through a 500mm lens set up on a tripod inside a vehicle. Arctic foxes commonly follow polar bears to capture lemmings disturbed by their passage on land or to scavenge their seal kills on the sea ice. A fox may range up to 1,000 miles away from its den in search of food, especially during periodic crashes of the lemming population. This natural wanderlust and curiosity has dispersed the arctic fox entirely around the Circumpolar North. The species reached America across the Bering Strait and quickly spread across all the islands of the Canadian High Arctic and up and down both coasts of Greenland. Despite intense trapping for their valuable fur, the species persists in the face of every sort of human encroachment, much like its more temperate canine cousin, the coyote. *(Nikon F4, 500mm f4 lens, f4 at 1/1000 second, Kodak Lumiere 100)*

Fuegian fox, Tierra del Fuego, Patagonia, Argentina; 1991 *p. 59*

The ubiquitous fox populates every continent except Antarctica and Australia, which lie across vast stretches of ocean that never freeze. The southernmost species is the Fuegian fox, or "Andean wolf," which lives on the island of Tierra del Fuego off the tip of South America. Its much larger size, compared with that of the related Patagonian fox on the mainland, may be an adaptation to its colder habitat, which falls within the zone of Antarctic climate as defined by the 50°F summer isotherm. Its ancestors crossed the Strait of Magellan during the ice ages, but probably failed to reach the Falkland Islands, where an extinct animal called the warrah that was exterminated by settlers in the 1870s was not a true fox, but most likely a descendant of a small feral dog. The cold-adapted Fuegian fox could undoubtedly survive on islands much farther south, but it would wreak havoc on wildlife. The enormous seabird colonies of the subantarctic sprawl across the type of open terrain that is prime hunting territory for a fox—and where an Arctic bird colony would therefore never nest. No continuous land masses penetrate the subantarctic seas, and no continuous pack ice has ever connected the more southerly islands in these rough waters to existing fox habitat. Ships do make this connection. Feral house cats released on a few islands south of the Antarctic Convergence give a hint of what might happen if foxes were introduced. Two cats were turned loose on Marion Island in 1949; 2,000 now kill half a million birds each year. On Kerguelen Island, cats take an estimated 1.2 million birds annually. I found this Fuegian fox far away from bird colonies, prowling in a thick beech forest. Other visitors to Tierra del Fuego National Park must have given it handouts, because it slowly approached me and virtually posed for its portrait as I set up my camera on a tripod at the edge of a small meadow. *(Nikon N90, 80–200mm f2.8 lens, f4 at 1/125 second, Fuji Velvia)*

Alaskan brown bear reaching for a salmon, Brooks Falls, Katmai National Park, Alaska; 1991 *p. 60*

The genetic similarity of brown and grizzly bears is due to their original circumpolar distribution. One subspecies, *Ursus arctos horribilis*, includes all the grizzlies of North America as well as the larger brown bear of the Alaskan coast, which crosses the threshold to a marine-based diet by feasting on salmon returning from the sea. Nineteenth-century zoologists described eighty-six species of grizzly and brown bears in separate enclaves without sensing a circumpolar overview. Europeans had eliminated *Ursus arctos* from most populated areas on their continent before Columbus, while Asiatic bears of the same species were gone from all but the most remote wilds of Siberia and the Himalaya. About 50,000 grizzlies were spread from California to Kansas in the early 1800s, but Francis Parkman's 1849 classic, *The Oregon Trail*, predicted a time when the plains of America "would be a grazing country, the buffalo give place to tame cattle, farmhouses be scattered along the water courses, and wolves, bears and Indians be numbered among the things that were." By the 1960s, when fewer than 1,000 seldom-seen grizzlies remained in this realm (although Alaska and Canada still had 40,000), Loren Eiseley wrote, "There is a need for a gentler man than those who won for us against the ice, the tiger, and the bear." Today, grizzly-viewing tourism has come into its own as human beings have begun to give up the urge to dominate nature and to recognize the great bear as symbolic of the natural condition of the North. I photographed this bear with a big lens on a tripod from an elevated deck 100 feet away. The platform was packed with people elbowing each other to defend enough territory to take photos, while commenting on the aggressive nature of the nine bears in the water, who bristled when a neighboring bear approached their prime fishing spot. *(Nikon F4, 500mm f4 lens, f4 at 1/1000 second, Fuji Velvia)*

Leopard seal, Paulet Island, Antarctic Peninsula; 1993 *p. 61*

The leopard seal's fierce reputation is well deserved if you happen to be a penguin or a young crabeater seal swimming near shore. From seemingly out of nowhere, you are grabbed by 1,000 pounds of long-necked killing machine with a wide-mouthed, reptilian look. Penguins are slit with sharp teeth and skinned inside out as they are snapped into the air. At an Adélie colony I visited on Cape Crozier, 4,800 adult penguins were taken by leopards in one season. About 80 percent of adult crabeater seals have leopard seal scars from when they were pups—a staggering number when you consider that crabeaters are the world's most numerous seals, estimated at over 14 million, while there are only half a million leopards.

Attacks on adult seals or humans are extremely rare. A penguin researcher recounted an eerie tale of being on an ice floe with an apparently oblivious leopard seal lying on the opposite side. Later, he noticed the seal was gone. No sooner did he take a step back than the seal erupted from the water, jaws open, precisely where he had been. It may have been a case of mistaken identity, for closer encounters are usually not aggressive. Underwater BBC cinematographers approached and filmed without incident two leopard seals engaged in what looks like an extended courtship ritual—but the myth continues, because the narration to their superb footage fails to mention that both seals were males. The seal in this photograph was prowling beside an Adélie penguin colony on Paulet Island. I lay flat on the pack ice with a telephoto lens to capture it looking like the solitary, subtle-spotted "sea-leopard" that early visitors so aptly described and named. *(Nikon F4, 80–200mm f2.8 lens, f5.6 at 1/250 second, Fuji Velvia)*

Inupiat Eskimo hunting seals on the frozen Arctic Ocean off Barrow, Alaska; 1994 *p. 62*

While cruising on a snowmobile across the sea ice with an Eskimo whaling crew en route to its camp, I stopped and got out my camera when our captain spotted a bearded seal at 500 yards. It was lying on the ice at the edge of an open lead of water. We shut off our engines and watched as the captain grabbed his rifle and began stalking the seal from the side, while we remained in place as decoys. I had previously been unable to get a single decent photograph of these wary animals on the ice, even with 1420mm of lens and teleconverters set up on a tripod. Thousands of years of intense hunting by Inuit natives and eons of predation by polar bears keep them ever on the alert, with their heads aimed toward the water for instant escape. I was surprised that this seal tolerated us at a distance, instead of dropping into the water within a second of spotting a human form, like all the others I had seen. The captain had neither the time nor the equipment for a typical Eskimo seal hunt, which can involve hours or days of staking out a breathing hole or approaching extremely slowly behind the camouflage of a white screen. When he came within 200 yards of the seal, it disappeared into the sea. I put away my long lens, but decided to frame a picture of his silhouette walking back in his outward track, wearing a white hunting parka that no longer served as camouflage against the snow, as he was backlit against the warm evening light. With a shorter telephoto braced on top of a nearby ice block, I caught him walking into the frame. *(Nikon N90, 80–200mm f2.8 lens, f5.6 at 1/60 second, Fuji Velvia push processed to ISO 100)*

Weddell seal's freezing breath at midnight near Cape Evans, Ross Island, Antarctica; 1992 *p. 63*

Unlike other southern seals that have been slaughtered for their fur or blubber, the Weddell's remote habitat has kept most human predators away. Here, the most southerly of the world's seals is about ready to give birth on the open ice at latitude 78° south. Compared with seals that live on Arctic ice, the Weddell exhibits virtually the opposite behavior when approached. Instead of fleeing, like Arctic seals, they stay sprawled on the ice and continue to sleep, unconcerned because they have no history of predation from either polar bears or people. This pregnant Weddell seal showed no fear whatsoever at my approach. I drove a small tracked vehicle called a Spryte within about 400 yards of her and walked in the open to within 100 yards, where I set up a tripod in plain view. I used a long telephoto lens in just the right position to catch the low-angled rays of the midnight sun illuminating her breath. The scene reminded me of an eloquent description of a similar encounter I had just read in David Campbell's book *The Crystal Desert*: "Her fur has water-drop markings that look like broad brushstrokes of Japanese silk painting. She is basking with her body aligned east and west in order to expose the maximum surface area to the sun's warmth. . . . The fluffed translucent hairs of the dry fur are traps for the sun's energy, converting visible light into infrared radiation and, by internal reflection, retaining it. Each hair is in effect a miniature greenhouse." *(Nikon F4, 300mm f2.8 lens, f8 at 1/8 second, Fuji Velvia)*

Trans-Alaska Pipeline crossing the Brooks Range near Atigun Pass, Alaska; 1993 *p. 64*

On my first visits to the pipeline, I never thought of composing a photograph anything like this one. I saw the pipeline several times in the seventies, both during and after its construction. Back then, I was overwhelmed by the sheer scope and impact of a human enterprise that rivaled the building of the Pyramids and the Great Wall of China. I placed this new apparition boldly in the foreground of my photographs. Biologists assured the Sierra Club that the declining Central Arctic Herd of caribou was in great danger of having its classic migration route interrupted. Workers' trucks sported bizarre juxtapositions of Tennessee plates beside "Sierra Go Home" bumper stickers. A compromise was negotiated to elevate the pipeline enough for animals to pass beneath in some areas or to construct ramps over the top where the pipe lay in or on the ground. To everyone's pleasant surprise, the herd proliferated to seven times its former size in two decades.

Before composing this photograph, I stood alone for long minutes, contemplating the tundra beneath my feet and the great silence of both the Brooks Range and the unseen 1.2 million barrels per day of liquid Devonian fossil that rush 800 miles from North America's largest oil-producing region through a 48-inch pipe to Valdez, from where tanker ships deliver the oil to a depot in San Francisco Bay near my home. I imagined the pipeline as an icon with a deeper meaning than its obvious presence and gave it some emotional distance from the foreground tundra. I switched to an extremely wide-angle lens with a curved field to create a stronger sense of this single line traversing the virgin landscape of the Circumpolar North. *(Nikon N90, 16mm f3.5 lens, f16 at 1/8 second, Fuji Velvia)*

Self-portrait among the flags of the Antarctic Treaty nations at the South Pole, Antarctica; 1992 *p. 65*

Before I arrived, I thought about making a photograph of the South Pole of the imagination using an extremely wide-angle lens to curve the bottom of the world as it appears from space. The National Science Foundation provided the perfect set: a circle of flags around a barber pole topped by a polished sphere. Pictures taken here of VIPs are often published without disclosing that this "Ceremonial South Pole"—200 feet from the official United States Geological Survey survey stakes (see page 132)—is not the true pole. The twelve flags represent the nations that originally signed the 1959 Antarctic Treaty: Argentina, Australia, Belgium, Chile, France, Japan, New Zealand, Norway, South Africa, the United Kingdom, the United States, and the Soviet Union. They agreed that Antarctica "shall continue forever to be used for peaceful purposes" as an outgrowth of scientific cooperation that had begun with the International Geophysical Year of 1957–58. Forty-two nations have now acceded to the treaty. An environmental protocol signed in 1991 designating Antarctica as a natural reserve is nearing ratification as of 1995. In contrast, the "Arctic Eight" nations—the United States, Canada, Denmark/Greenland, Iceland, Norway, Sweden, Finland, and Russia—have yet to agree on anything remotely similar, although an emerging "Arctic Environmental Protection Strategy" is far enough along to mention here in capital letters. The Arctic Eight have permanent residents, economic priorities, indigenous people, and long-established borders to worry about, but Antarctic altruism also has its limitations. An 85-year-old British major, who met a member of Scott's 1911 expedition as a boy, became the oldest visitor to both poles in 1993. The Americans at their South Pole station turned him outside as an uninvited guest to spend three -35°F nights in a tent after bad weather had grounded his private flight. The NSF policy of not supporting private expeditions is widely known. *(Nikon N90, 16mm f3.5 lens, f22 at 1/15 second, Fuji Velvia)*

Inupiat Eskimo whalers with bomb guns, Arctic Ocean, near Barrow, Alaska; 1994 *p. 66*

Two members of a whaling crew hold bomb guns designed to quickly kill a bowhead whale moments after it has been harpooned. One reason that the Eskimo community is cautious about allowing outsiders to witness hunts is that casual observers might jump to the wrong conclusion that the use of such weapons during an otherwise traditional endeavor is inhumane. To the contrary, the old ways caused more suffering. The quicker death from a delayed charge set off deep within the whale is a key factor in continued permissions for subsistence hunting.

The development of the maritime culture that allowed coastal Eskimos to survive in such an extreme environment for untold millennia was directly tied to bowhead whaling. Beyond the supply of the whale meat and the festivals that follow successful hunts, whaling accounts for the use of baleen for creative works of art, the winter tradition of groups of women stitching sealskins together to cover umiaks, and the hunt itself as a training ground—out on the fickle sea ice or in an open boat—for traditional survival skills and methods of hunting other animals. Eskimos hunted bowheads for thousands of years before the animals became rapidly endangered by European and American commercial whaling, which ended in the early 1900s. Since then, bowhead numbers in the Bering Sea have increased to about 8,000. Gray whales that occasionally visit Barrow are not part of the Eskimo hunt. The famous 1988 incident in which two gray whales stuck in the ice off Barrow were freed after extraordinary effort and media coverage was the result of an Eskimo named Roy Ahmaogak reporting whales in trouble. *(Nikon N90, 35–70 f2.8 lens, f5.6 at 1/60 second, Fuji Velvia)*

Gurkha soldiers at Grytviken, South Georgia Island, Subantarctic; 1993 *p. 67*

In the abandoned whaling village of Grytviken, I came across elephant seals sleeping atop whale-processing apparatus and fresh white letters painted by Greenpeace on storage tanks to show the quantity of whale oil that still remained. Most incongruous, however, was coming face-to-face with two armed Gurkha soldiers, even though I knew that a small garrison of British soldiers was stationed there. I looked them in the eye, smiled, and said, "*Namaste.*" They smiled back with surprise at my greeting in their own language. I learned that both were from the Arun Valley of Nepal beneath Mount Everest. They were touched to learn that I had trekked and climbed on Mount Everest. As they gladly posed for a portrait holding their assault weapons, I used a "smart flash" on automatic exposure to fill just enough light on the soldiers to balance with the ambient light.

The British began hiring Nepalese hill tribesmen as mercenary soldiers in the early nineteenth century. The forty-five Gurkha battalions that fought during World War II were noted for extreme bravery. Legend has it that half a Gurkha regiment stepped forward when a British officer wanted volunteers for a risky 1,000-foot airdrop behind enemy lines. As the mission was further explained, a soldier asked, "You mean we can use parachutes?" Then the other half stepped forward. In 1982, Gurkha soldiers played a key role in the British victory in the Falklands war, especially after the Argentine press belittled them as a cross between dwarfs and mountain goats. South Georgia became the only part of the Antarctic region ever directly involved in a war when Argentine gunships seized a scientific station and took British prisoners. Gurkhas have been stationed on the island ever since. *(Nikon N90, 35–70 f2.8 lens, SB-25 flash, f5.6 at 1/60 second, Fuji Velvia)*

Commercial seal hunt, Pribilof Islands, Bering Sea, Alaska; 1979 *p. 68*

While riding a Honda Trail 90 motorbike to photograph a bird colony at the far end of Saint Paul Island, I came across a group of Aleuts herding northern fur seals into an open field and clubbing them to death. They didn't look pleased when I got off the motorbike I had rented from the local pastor and took out my camera. I hesitated using the tripod in my backpack because I thought the appearance of professional photography might create an incident. Greenpeace, the Fund for Animals, and the Humane Society had spoken out against the annual commercial harvest of 30,000 seals, but I had no special agenda. Although I don't like mass killing, the seals weren't endangered and government literature emphasized a stable population of over a million.

The Aleuts looked unfriendly as I walked over to a row of fresh skins and took a few handheld shots with a wide-angle lens. Although the hunt was a family affair, no one looked happy. The atmosphere was very different in fact from that of the Eskimo subsistence hunts I later witnessed, where men on the ice seemed deeply satisfied to be living out their traditional heritage, whether or not their hunt was successful. The Aleuts are not native to the Pribilofs. They were first brought as slaves to kill and skin seals by the Russian fur trader Gerassim Pribilof, who in 1786 discovered the world's largest concentration of mammals and seabirds on the uninhabited islands. After the purchase of Alaska in 1867, the Aleuts became more or less wards of the U.S. government until 1983, when they gained control of the islands but lost the direct government sanction that had allowed them to pursue commercial sealing. Although subsistence hunts continue to a limited degree, Aleut claims to traditional or subsistence hunting on the Pribilofs pale beside those of the coastal Eskimos. *(Nikon FM, 24mm f2.8 lens, f5.6 at 1/15 second, Kodachrome 64)*

153

Whaling protest sign in Port Stanley backyard, Falkland Islands; 1993 *p. 69*
During the first half of the twentieth century, the Falklands were a major hub for the most prolific whaling on the planet. Up to 10,000 whales per year were killed in the subantarctic seas of the Falkland Islands Dependencies. The power of the pro-whaling lobby, like that of the National Rifle Association, proves itself in the conspicuous absence of regulations in key documents. Thus the original 1959 Antarctic Treaty does not mention whaling activities or other resource issues. Until recently, the International Whaling Commission has failed to successfully regulate whaling in the deep South. When I made this photograph, the IWC was contemplating a Southern Ocean Whale Sanctuary to include all waters below latitude 40° south. Within months, the sanctuary was created, but with a gaping wedge exempting the Falklands, the tip of South America, and the most-visited subantarctic waters down to latitude 60° south.

As I walked through Port Stanley, I purposely didn't photograph this sign at first, because I didn't want to copy a somewhat different picture of it made by Colin Monteath, a fellow photographer and Antarctic guide. The fenced backyard faces a main street, and on my way back, I was greeted by a cheery hello from a man in his eighties working in the garden. When I asked him about the sign, he told me that the time had come to speak out for preserving the last remaining great whales. His father had been a whaler who had emigrated from the United Kingdom. He was pleased to pose for a photograph that would emphasize his personal message, and he helped me find a box to stand on to compose an unusual downward perspective on the sign with a handheld wide-angle lens. I asked him to step into the frame and tell me about his life. *(Nikon N90, 24mm f2.8 lens, f11 at 1/30 second, Fuji Velvia)*

Inupiat Eskimo harpooning a bowhead whale, Arctic Ocean, near Barrow, Alaska; 1994 *p. 70*
It all happened in a moment. We were on a bench covered with caribou skins beside the ice edge when an Eskimo beside me pointed to ripples on the surface a few hundred feet away, moving slowly toward us. Without a word, the crew of five launched their umiak and jumped inside in one fluid motion. I watched through my viewfinder as the captain, Thomas Brower III, raised his harpoon and aimed it toward a whale right beside his boat. He never threw the harpoon. "Would have lost that one," he said as he came ashore. "Headed under the ice." After a repeat performance within the hour, all was still again. It was my last day. I had been out on the ice for a week with the crew, watching them chase about a dozen whales through lenses up to 1420mm. Forty crews were out and only one whale had been caught.

Thomas III is the great-grandson of Charles Brower, a whaler who married an Eskimo and became Barrow's first white resident in 1893. Thomas III was seven when he began whaling with his father. After more than thirty years of apprenticeship, he formed his own crew and became a captain. I first met him on a winter trip when he posed for photos without the slightest impatience on a breezy evening when the chill factor was -70°F. When I asked to join his crew I didn't know that he had never personally caught a whale. Late on my last day on the ice, he slipped from the bench into the boat again and harpooned this one right beside me as I snapped away with a handheld camera at a high shutter speed to freeze the action. *(Nikon F4, 80–200mm f2.8 lens, f4 at 1/1000 second, Fuji Velvia push processed to ISO 100)*

Killer whales in Paradise Bay, Antarctic Peninsula; 1992 *p. 71*
When we arrived in glacier-draped Paradise Bay, dark clouds hung over absolutely still water without a breath of wind. Our relatively small Russian research vessel, *Professor Molchanov*, hardly disturbed the idyllic scene as we lowered Zodiac rafts into the black, plankton-rich waters to cruise around. Minutes later, a large group of Adélie penguins porpoised past us at full speed, headed for land. Then came a black dorsal fin moving rapidly in the distance. Soon four more fins appeared, and we caught a glimpse of contrasting black and white as a large male killer whale momentarily surfaced. The pod of five cruised the bay for several minutes, missing the penguins, but coming close to another raft as I made this shot with the longest lens in my bag—280mm of 80–200mm zoom plus a 1.4x teleconverter. As the pod approached us, one whale dove under our raft, coming up in a wake that nearly dumped my cameras into the sea and made low-light photography impossible until the shaking ceased and the whales were gone.

Killer whales, also known by their scientific name, *orca*, are extremely intelligent and social members of the dolphin family. They often eat penguins and seals, but despite chilling tales of close calls, no human has ever been attacked by an unprovoked killer whale, to the best of my knowledge. In fact, the killer whales have more to fear from us, especially since the Russians began to kill them in the 1970s in the subantarctic after depleting stocks of blue, fin, and sei whales. The new 1994 Southern Ocean Whale Sanctuary, plus a tourism code of conduct recently adopted by the Antarctic Treaty nations, should help perpetuate scenes like this. *(Nikon F4, 80–200mm f2.8 lens with 1.4x teleconverter, f4 at 1/500 second, Fuji Velvia push processed to ISO 100)*

Young Inupiat Eskimo woman in winter furs, Barrow, Alaska; 1994 *p. 72*
A strong gust of wind tugs at the warm ruff of wolf and wolverine that keeps this young woman smiling in April at latitude 71° north. Predator furs resist ice buildup from breath better than those of caribou or the synthetic materials introduced in recent years. Fine fur parkas such as this are reserved for special occasions, but even the most simple cotton or nylon winter parka an Eskimo might wear to school or the grocery store usually has a well-chosen fur ruff for comfort and insulation. The day I made this photograph, the newspaper published a report from the Eskimo town of Anaktuvuk: "Today is 40 below, clear, good sunshine. People have been going out on picnics. They go someplace, maybe 5–10 miles out, build a bonfire, and cook some hamburgers and drink hot tea."

The *Inupiat* people of Barrow would rather be called *Eskimo*, a name from their own language, than *Inuit*, the politically correct alternative chosen by their Canadian cousins. French-Canadian trappers originally bastardized *Esquimaux* from an Algonquian word meaning *eater of raw flesh*. At least the more specific term refers to the entire loose-knit group of circumpolar native Arctic peoples who speak dialects of the same language and have banded together at international meetings to work for preservation of their ancient cultures.

Barbara Rexford's open smile is a direct counterpoint to the sullen attitude of one Eskimo out on the ice who told me, "As far as I'm concerned, you don't exist. My people owe you nothing. You are here because your government illegally bought us and our land from another government that had no right to sell us and barely knew of our existence. We weren't part of the Alaskan territory that Russia controlled in 1867." *(Nikon N90, 80–200mm f2.8 lens, f4 at 1/500 second, Fuji Velvia)*

Tim Cully on top of Mount Erebus, Ross Island, Antarctica; 1992 *p. 73*

Tim Cully's high-tech synthetic clothing worked well for active scrambling around the summit of an Antarctic mountain on a -32°F evening. As he sweated from exertion, moisture wicked from the polypropylene against his body through another layer of acrylic pile. Most of it was released into the cold atmosphere through a final shell of windproof but breathable Gore-tex. Were Tim to sit down for the night without tent or sleeping bag, he would get extremely cold—or worse. I wore the same type of garments as Tim and stayed warm by keeping moving. We were both well aware of the limitations of the trade-off we were making. We could move quickly, but our garments lacked the insulation value of traditional Eskimo furs that are designed for living in the cold. Ours were conceived, sold, and mostly worn by people who do special tasks in the cold, knowing they will return to a heated room. I took this photo to show the ice buildup on Tim's face as well as his many layers of clothing and face shielding.

In 1911, Roald Amundsen's first successful expedition to the South Pole used suits of Lapp reindeer skins sown into Eskimo-style garments worn over woolens. He came from Norway, a nation that reaches into the Arctic and has a solid tradition of polar explorations using native garments and dogs. Robert Falcon Scott's tragic expedition from non-Arctic Britain consciously avoided dogs and furs. His team used mostly gabardine, canvas, and a few woolens to reach the pole a month after Amundsen. They starved and froze to death on the return. Before the trip, Scott had written, "We find not only that furs are unnecessary for winter wear, but can't imagine that they would be otherwise than positively objectionable." *(Nikon N90, 35–70mm f2.8 lens, f8 at 1/125, Fuji Velvia)*

Aerial view of Scoresbysund, northeast Greenland; 1993 *p. 74*

The village of Scoresbysund displays the pleasing coherence of Scandinavian architecture well beyond the Arctic Circle at latitude 70° north. Ninety percent of its 500 residents are Inuit; the remainder, Danes. After two centuries of Danish control, native Greenlanders were given home rule in 1979. Their acquired tastes for neat frame houses with white trim, commercial fishing, and European-style education for their children continue, however, thanks to millions of dollars of Danish assistance each year that pays for imported goods and social services. In 1985, the new Greenland flexed its muscles and voted to leave the European Economic Community to better protect its fishing rights, thus cutting in half the land area of the EEC.

Beneath Scoresbysund's benign appearance from the air is a wild native village with high rates of violent crime, alcoholism, and suicide. Beneath the snows that melt back during the short summers, the town is littered with trash. The days when Greenland Inuit lived a slower subsistence lifestyle in sod houses out in meadows where the flowers bloom in June are not that far in the past. The ice-free edge of the northeast coast above the Arctic Circle has been called the Arctic Riviera because of its fine summer climate. However, the region has a history of mysterious disappearances. The Thule people, who inhabited the northeast coast for thousands of years, were last seen by Douglas Clavering's 1823 British scientific expedition, but never again. After the winter of 1899, the caribou disappeared, and the wolves soon followed.

I flew over Scoresbysund on my way to Northeast Greenland National Park on a perfect October day just after the fjord, which extends 180 miles into the interior, had frozen. I asked the pilot to do a slow circle as I shot out an open window in the cockpit at both the town and the mountains that rose out of the deep fjord. *(Nikon N90, 35mm f1.4 lens with polarizing filter, f1.4 at 1/1000, Fuji Velvia)*

McMurdo Station, Ross Island, Antarctica; 1992 *p. 75*

I framed this overview from Arrival Heights, high above "Mac Town," as the major U.S. station is called by some of its 1,600 seasonal residents. The station clearly lacks the pleasing distant appearance of Scoresbysund, but on close inspection it has a high degree of workaday neatness thanks to an intense recycling operation and attention to litter. No one group or individual has been accountable for McMurdo's aesthetically challenged appearance. The National Science Foundation has run the U.S. Antarctic Research Program since 1955, but received full responsibility for operational aspects only in 1972. McMurdo is also the base for field support from the U.S. Navy, the U.S. Coast Guard, and an NSF contractor—presently Antarctic Support Associates—that supplies staff to handle daily operations as well as to assist scientists in the field. Most everyone finds humor in unofficial "McMurdo Happens" bumper stickers posted on vehicles and walls, but a complete fix will take years. The seed of the problem can be seen a few miles away at Ernest Shackleton's 1907 hut, kept as he left it by a provision of the Antarctic Treaty. Against a wall is a pile of perfectly preserved cans and bottles atop the frozen ground. Imagine how it would look if 1,600 explorers had lived there for forty years.

In 1993, a team of architects invited to McMurdo by NSF to develop a future planning strategy observed how "McMurdo has evolved in response to changing demands for supply and support . . . within a harness of stringent political and financial restraints," thus creating "a mixture of overlapping functions, resulting in a jumble of science facilities, housing, community services, and materials handling." They suggested ways to reduce energy use for heating by 50 percent and to create a visual aesthetic in line with "the station's purpose of research and its compatibility with the natural environment." In 1994, the NSF had two master planners on its contract staff working out methods to cut water and energy use in half. *(Nikon F4, 35–70mm f2.8 lens, f11 at 1/60 second, Fuji Velvia)*

Chukchi whalebone structure, Arakamchechen Island, Chukchi Peninsula, Siberia; 1993 *p. 76*

When I spotted bowhead whale ribs as tall as a two-story house standing on the shore of Arakamchechen Island, I saw a photo possibility that was not yet before my eyes. Beneath a cloudy sky, the bones were as flat and bluish as the sea. Size cues were absent. A snapshot taken at the time would be something we show only our friends with a disclaimer: "It was really much bigger and more impressive. I guess you had to be there." I was reluctant to put myself in the scene beside the bones as scale because to do so would have intruded on the very sanctity I wanted to capture—an ancient space frozen in time. When two members of my group walked into the picture I was carefully composing in perfect sunset light, I asked them to stand still for a minute right in the center of my frame, at a distance that conveyed respect for the ancient artifact as well as scale.

Chukchi Eskimos had placed the ribs as supports for a long-gone home hundreds of years ago. They had survived for generations by catching fish, seals, walrus, and the occasional bowhead whale until foreign ships began to come in the 1700s, rapidly depleting their marine resources. Their early history is unwritten, and they were the last Siberian natives to accede to Russia. My group had also visited "Whalebone Alley" on nearby Yttygran Island, where old structures like this one are interspersed with bowhead skulls precisely aligned to form patterns reminiscent of the giant stones of Easter Island. Some anthropologists believe the Chukchis used them to measure the months by the path of the sun and determine the solstice. Modern Chukchis, who live in ugly towns set up as communes by the Soviets, were aware of the shrines, but thought little of them until their "discovery" in 1976 by a Russian scientific expedition. *(Nikon N90, 80–200mm f2.8 lens, f16 at 1/4 second, Fuji Velvia)*

155

Perfectly preserved interior of Shackleton's Hut, Cape Royds, Antarctica; 1992 *p. 77*

Ernest Shackleton built this hut in 1907 during the first expedition to declare the South Pole as its main objective. He came within 97 nautical miles, closer than many experts believe Robert Peary came to the North Pole just six months later.

When I stepped into the hut, which looked as if Shackleton had slept there the night before, I instantly knew that the modern photographs I had seen do not do the place justice and that, despite my special preparations to capture as much as possible on film, mine would not hold that tangible immediacy of stepping into the past either. We sense that even the newest photograph freezes a moment in the past, and we are also used to seeing very old photographs. The difference between photographs of this hut taken in 1908 and in 1992 could be slight, while actually viewing a place frozen in time is powerfully different from viewing either photograph.

Since 1959, New Zealanders at Scott Base have overseen the preservation of the locked hut. While working with the National Science Foundation, I was given the key with the dire warning that if anything was disturbed or moved out of place, I would be on the next flight home. I arrived in early spring when drifted snow still covered the sides of the building and blocked the light from the windows. After digging a hole outside to let a beam of sunlight hit the floor, I used a folding reflector to "paint" the room with light. I first held the beam in one spot to take a light reading. After estimating a 20-second exposure for the room, I then moved the beam like a brush. A special rectilinear 15mm lens rendered straight lines without distortion in a broad field of view. *(Nikon F4, 15mm f3.5 lens, f5.6 at 20 seconds, Fuji Velvia)*

The "Hickel Highway" leading into Gates of the Arctic National Park, Brooks Range, Alaska; 1993 *p. 78*

Most Americans don't realize that the period of the late sixties and early seventies in Alaska were almost as tumultuous as the Bolshevik Revolution was for its Siberian neighbors. Social, political, economic, and environmental upheaval radically changed the pattern of land ownership of vast wild areas of the state as the "last frontier" closed at a rate unprecedented in American history. A tenth of the state's land and a billion dollars were given to the natives, while another quarter of the state was designated for federal protection that eventually tripled the size of the nation's wilderness areas and doubled that of national park and wildlife refuges. One of these areas in limbo was the region soon to become Gates of the Arctic National Park and Preserve. In 1966, disposition of Alaskan federal lands was frozen by the Secretary of the Interior. When oil was discovered on the North Slope in 1968, Governor Walter Hickel, knowing that oil money would transform his state government into one with unprecedented power, felt that exploration could not wait for equipment to be shipped to the Arctic after the pack ice melted the following summer. He wanted to build a highway across the Brooks Range to Prudhoe Bay, but environmentalists objected. He compromised with what became known as the "Hickel Highway," a temporary winter route following traditional wilderness trails upon which trucks would drive atop the snow-covered frozen ground, so as not to harm the fragile organic mat of the tundra. Although the route was soon abandoned, a prominent scar remained clearly visible from the air a quarter century later, when I flew over it with my camera held out the open window of Vern Kingsford's Cessna 172. *(Nikon F4, 35mm f1.4 lens, f1.4 at 1/1000 second, Fuji Velvia push processed to ISO 100)*

Gentoo penguins nesting in a bombed-out Argentine science base, Thule Island, South Sandwich Islands, Subantarctic; 1993 *p. 79*

On our way back from the first tourist voyage into the Weddell Sea, our icebreaker made an unscheduled stop at Thule Island, the southernmost of the South Sandwich Islands. Since the weather was very poor at our other destinations in the group—the symmetrical volcano of Candlemas and the world's largest penguin colony of Zavadovsky Island—our captain bided time by stopping at a place that seemed to have no special merit. When the islands were discovered by Captain Cook in 1774, he described the chain as a worthless, doomed place "whose horrible and savage aspects I have not words to describe." After we landed Zodiac rafts beneath the ruins of an Argentine scientific base, I came across this poignant scene of penguins nesting in the toxic mess that no one had cleaned up. With a wide-angle lens, I composed a twisted girder to lead the viewer's eye through the frame.

Both the British and the Argentines had claimed the South Sandwich group, but nothing happened until the Argentines attacked South Georgia during the Falklands war of 1982. The British weren't about to leave, because their land claims on the Antarctic continent are based upon ownership of subantarctic islands abeam those lands. A staff member on our trip, David Rootes, had heard rumors of the destruction when he managed a British subantarctic base in the South Orkney Islands. Legend had it that the Argentines were removed at gunpoint from this base when they lost the war, but someone later ran their flag up the pole—possibly a prank by a passing ship. When a British warship on patrol saw an Argentine flag flying, the captain radioed London and was instructed to destroy the base immediately. The Antarctic Treaty forbids military actions south of latitude 60°, but Thule is at 59°30's, just outside that line, yet south of the Antarctic Convergence and thus biologically part of Antarctica. Not to have cleaned up the mess ten years later is unforgivable. *(Nikon N90, 24mm f2.8 lens, f16 at 1/8 second, Fuji Velvia)*

Nuclear ship base at Murmansk, Russian Arctic; 1993 *p. 80*

Until 1991, this base was top secret and off-limits to visitors. That summer, passengers from the first tourist voyage to the North Pole were taken off the ship by helicopter before it docked. Two years later, I was uncertain how we would disembark and if we could take photographs. We landed at night, and just before dawn I tried to walk off the gangplank and was stopped by a guard. We had not been cleared by customs. I returned with a camera under my jacket mounted on a small tripod. No one paid any attention as I set it up before the gangplank and took several long time exposures. The strange, unfiltered colors are the result of the mixtures of ambient and artificial light.

When we disembarked, the vessel docked beside us took me by surprise. The *Lenin*, the very first nuclear icebreaker, commissioned in 1959, had been towed to its present location in 1968, a year after suffering a reactor meltdown in the Arctic seas that killed between twenty-seven and thirty people. The ship had been too contaminated to move for a year. Greenpeace reports that another of Russia's nine nuclear icebreakers came very close to suffering a meltdown while docked at Murmansk in 1988 after a physicist gave "an erroneous command."

Murmansk, the largest city north of the Arctic Circle, has a population of over half a million, equal to the entire state of Alaska. The key to its growth is the Russian development of the Northern Sea Route—also called the Northeast Passage. The old government invested all the necessary resources to keep the shipping lanes open with nuclear icebreakers to the city's ice-free port, which became known to the Western world during World War II as the year-round Arctic delivery port for Allied support of Russia. *(Nikon N90, 20mm f2.8 lens, f4 at 15 seconds, Fuji Velvia)*

Private fuel cache at the South Pole, Antarctica; 1992 *p. 81*

The strangest sight I saw at the South Pole was this abandoned fuel cache of Chilean drums with a sign pointing to Mecca in both Arabic and English. I spotted it as I was returning with John Lynch of the National Science Foundation from photographing a crashed LC-130 Hercules aircraft just past the end of the runway. The accident had happened over twenty years earlier, and the wreck had been towed into position as a navigation aid in the middle of the ice to bounce back radar from planes landing in poor visibility. Whereas the plane was entirely buried in drifting snow with just the tail showing, the cache was in much better shape. John told me that it had been left during Will Steger's International Trans-Antarctica Expedition of 1989–90. The expedition had been in danger of failure because a fuel cache promised and paid for in advance was not delivered by a private adventure company that was having logistical problems. Of course, the NSF station at the pole had fuel, but the U.S. government has a strict policy of no support whatsoever to private adventurers except in emergencies serious enough to threaten personal safety. Aid is given only on condition that a team abort further travel and be evacuated at its own expense. Will Steger made calls on his radio and arranged for 12 tons of fuel from a Soviet expedition to be brought to the pole by Twin Otter aircraft. One of his sponsors was His Royal Highness, Prince Sultan bin Abdul Aziz of Saudi Arabia. In the plane that brought the fuel were also two Saudi oceanographers, who were responsible for the sign left atop the remaining fuel, which had come from a depot used by both the Russians and the Chileans. No one wants to deal with the legal ramifications of altering or removing the private cache, which is worth at least $7,500 per full barrel of fuel. *(Nikon F4, 24mm f2.8 lens, f16 at 1/30 second, Fuji Velvia)*

Atmospheric physicist monitoring Arctic haze, Barrow, Alaska; 1994 *p. 82*

The Barrow Baseline Observatory is part of a global surface air sampling program for the National Oceanic and Atmospheric Administration, along with three other baseline observatories at the South Pole, Mauna Loa, and Samoa. I had roamed through the Barrow facility for an hour, trying to make a single photograph to sum up the purpose of the esoteric equipment that surrounded me, when Daniel Endres, the station chief, showed me a jet black filter removed after one week of sampling 53 cubic feet of outside air per minute. I asked him to hold it up beside a fresh white filter while I stood on a ladder above him and shot with an ultra-wide 16mm lens.

Within days of the 1986 Chernobyl nuclear disaster, Barrow became the first place in America to detect fallout. The observatory found greatly increased levels of beryllium, iridium, cesium, and rubidium as part of a U.S. Department of Energy cooperative program to monitor radionuclides.

The first reports of distinct brownish layers of dirty air over the Arctic came from bush pilots. Commercial jets on polar routes often report tenfold drops in visibility inside haze layers. The importance of Arctic haze is not its quantity so much as its role as a conduit for toxic materials from the south. Combined ground and flight air sampling has charted the clear path of pollutants from Eurasia all the way across the North Pole into Alaska. Trace amounts of vanadium from the burning of fossil fuels greatly increase in haze, for example, as do much larger amounts of sulfuric acid and methane. Some of the airborne material is of natural origin. A major sandstorm in the deserts north of the Himalaya can send half a million tons of particulates over Alaska. Arctic air may be 200 times less clear than air at the South Pole, but peak values are still below those on average days over my hometown of Berkeley, California. *(Nikon F4, 16mm f3.5 lens, f16 at 2 seconds, Fuji Velvia)*

NASA scientist Don Barch remotely operating a Mars analog robotic vehicle, Antarctica; 1992 *p. 83*

I spent an intriguing week in the McMurdo Dry Valleys with scientists from merging disciplines. Dr. Robert Wharton, a research professor specializing in desert biology, believes that life in the ice-covered freshwater lakes of this polar desert offers a terrestrial analog for life that may have existed long ago on Mars. The mean annual temperature on Mars is -20°F, not that far from the -4°F of the Dry Valleys. Evidence of ancient water, atmosphere, and geothermal activity on the red planet ups the odds. While NASA researchers were using the extreme environment as a proving ground for remote control of camera-equipped robotic vehicles on Mars, Wharton was able to explore the biological, chemical, and physical characteristics of the waters of Lake Hoare. The project demonstrates the feasibility of controlling robots on Mars by telepresence, which operates by closely coupling human perceptions and gestures to robotic actions taking place elsewhere. Although telepresence is a step below full virtual reality, where things happen in "real time" with no delay, I felt an out-of-body experience when I donned the head-mounted display. Through the fiber optics, I could see only what was happening elsewhere; when I turned my head left, the camera turned left as if I were indeed right there.

NASA was testing the feasibility of sending a robot to Mars on an unmanned mission in which the robot leaves the landing site and "mines" the thin Mars atmosphere to stockpile 108 tons of methane and liquid oxygen. This fuel would power the return voyage of a lightweight manned mission, months later, which would not have to carry the heavy payload of return fuel all the way to Mars. The radical plan is an attempt to save the NASA Mars project by cutting $350 billion of the $400 billion program, which lost its congressional funding. *(Nikon N90, 80–200mm f2.8 lens, f8 at 1/250 second, Fuji Velvia)*

Russian nuclear icebreaker *Yamal* at 89° north en route to the North Pole; 1993 *p. 84*

A brand-new Russian icebreaker, in service less than a year, transports a group of Quark Expeditions tourists to the North Pole, cruising at 14 knots through 6 feet of pack ice. To make this photograph, I had one of the two onboard helicopters drop me on the ice 2 miles ahead of the ship; there, I set up a 600mm lens to capture the ship looming toward me from a safe distance. The ship's 75,000 horsepower sometimes generated cracks up to half a mile ahead that split the ice amidst a cacophony of snaps and booms. Curious polar bears hundreds of miles from land were drawn toward the ship at latitudes up to 83° north.

The first surface ship to reach the North Pole was a Soviet nuclear vessel called the *Arktika* in 1977. For a decade afterward, no other surface ships made the journey. Ship-based tourism to the pole began in 1991 with a Quark-chartered journey for just over 100 passengers on the *Yamal's* sister ship, the *Sovetskiy Soyuz.* Four other tourist voyages on nuclear ships had been made by the time of our trip in 1993. We began in the Bering Strait opposite Alaska and traversed the entire Northern Sea Route above Siberia before veering north to the pole, south to rescue the trapped *Kapitan Khlebnikov* off the northern tip of Greenland, and back across the top of Svalbard with a detour to Franz Josef Land before disembarking at the nuclear base in Murmansk, the largest city in the world beyond either the Arctic or Antarctic Circle. *(Nikon F4, 300mm f2.8 AFI lens with 2X teleconverter, f5.6 at 1/250 second, Fuji Velvia)*

Russian diesel icebreaker *Kapitan Khlebnikov* in pack ice of the Weddell Sea, Antarctica; 1993 *p. 85*

A working Russian icebreaker, normally used for trade on the Northern Sea Route above Siberia, has rammed into the pack ice to allow passengers to walk to a nearby emperor penguin colony (see page 108). An Australian travel entrepreneur chartered the ship for Quark Expeditions to make the first tourist voyage into the heart of the Weddell Sea, where Sir Ernest Shackleton's ship, the *Endurance*, sank in 1915 after getting trapped in the pack ice. Shackleton's epic rescue of all twenty-eight men on board, who floated on rafts of ice and an open boat for a year and a half, is one of the greatest survival stories of all time.

Just three months before I took this photograph, the *Kapitan Khlebnikov* had been stuck in the ice while attempting the first circumnavigation of Greenland. I had been returning from the North Pole on the nuclear icebreaker *Yamal* when we received a radio message calmly saying there was no emergency, but the ship was unable to move and needed assistance. We aborted our itinerary, crossed an uncharted part of the Arctic Ocean, and broke the ship loose four days later. Times have changed in the seventy-eight years since Shackleton's epic. We found it fascinating to retrace much of Shackleton's route, but our journey was far more interesting as one of the world's great natural history itineraries. One can hardly blame Shackleton for not reporting in depth on the birds and marine mammals his men encountered as they fought for their lives. In this photograph, passengers are disembarking onto 6 feet of pack ice at latitude 71° south. I got off first to position myself on the ground before the ship with a 20mm wide-angle lens pointed up toward the bow to depict its massive scale against the tiny figures. *(Nikon N90, 20mm f4 lens, f8 at 1/30 second, Fuji Velvia)*

Northern lights over winter camp in the Brooks Range, Alaska; 1994 *p. 86*

While on a 100-mile journey by dog team into Gates of the Arctic National Park, we camped on a knoll in a spruce forest on a clear night. Our yellow "Arctic Oven" tents equipped with small woodstoves and bright lanterns provided objects of warm light to complement the blue tones of night and the vivid green of the northern lights, or aurora borealis, which began to dance around the sky like shimmering curtains across an open window at about 9 P.M. Staying up on a perfect Arctic winter night was not hard duty. I would set a two-minute exposure on the timer of a special battery-powered Nikon remote cable, grab a cup of hot chocolate, and watch the motion of the lights that I couldn't capture. When I heard the shutter close, I would wait for the right moment to try again. Several members of my group stayed up with me until midnight, when the lights weakened and virtually disappeared. Although many photographers use fast film to freeze shapes with as little motion as possible, I wanted a more open feeling on finer-grained film that would show the lights more in balance with a finely rendered night landscape. I used relatively slow film with my camera on a sturdy tripod while I compromised and waited for displays that would hold long diagonals for a period of time. I depressed my shutter at times when the lights moved more slowly at the end of an arc across the sky.

During the International Geophysical Year of 1957–58, researchers proved that auroras are conjugate—in other words, at the same moment, auroras of similar shape and duration occur in both polar regions at opposite ends of a magnetic field line. Displays of the aurora borealis in Alaska tend to be brighter than elsewhere in the Arctic, or in the Antarctic, where they are called aurora australis. *(Nikon N90, 35mm f1.4 lens, f1.4 at 2 minutes, Kodak Lumiere 100 push processed to ISO 200)*

Midnight on Ice Tower Ridge, Mount Erebus, Ross Island, Antarctica; 1992 *p. 87*

Just below the rim of the crater of this active volcano, a row of smoking ice towers rises up to 80 feet above the ground. The towers gradually freeze around steam fumaroles and increase in size until every few years a big blow topples them. Meanwhile, the inside air temperature stabilizes at just above freezing as the diameter of the cold ice tube grows to match the volume of warm air passing upward. Besides being the most active Antarctic volcano, Mount Erebus has been in a continuously eruptive state at least since the turn of the century, when members of Scott's and Shackleton's expeditions frequently witnessed spectacular displays in the polar night.

Survival guide Tim Cully and I spent an entire early spring night exploring the ice towers while the sun remained just above the horizon. Tim stood beside the largest tower with ice ax in hand while I carefully composed the scene with a natural diffraction star coming off the tower beside him, caused by the sun's rays bending around the edge. Note that the sun is too high above the horizon to justify the degree of pink tones near the horizon, yet no colored filter was used. The cause of the diffuse salmon-colored ring around the sun in 1992 was the "Pinatubo effect" of light scattered in the stratosphere after the huge eruption of the equatorial volcano the previous year. In a normal year, the lighting would have been harsh, cool, and contrasty. Although my shutter speed wasn't so slow that I needed a tripod, I used one anyway to hold precise composition while I bracketed multiple exposures and used slightly different camera positions to get just the right silhouette and sun star on the left to balance against the deep blue sky on the other side of the frame. *(Nikon N90, 20mm f4 lens, f8 at 1/30 second, Fuji Velvia)*

Dog team heading into Gates of the Arctic National Park, Brooks Range, Alaska; 1994 *p. 90*

Like riding horses in the American West, mushing your own team of dogs across the frozen tundra strikes a chord far deeper than merely traveling across the land. Days on the trail take you back to a time when people formed bonds with the domestic animals they depended on for transportation—and their very survival—in the roadless wilds.

Once the classic means of Arctic transportation, dogsledding as a way of life has almost vanished in Alaska, except for racing and adventure tourism. Since the 1970s, Sourdough Outfitters of Bettles has been teaching novices to run their own teams through the roadless Brooks Range. When I joined one of their expeditions, I didn't believe my guide's comment that everyone should expect white knuckles at first, until I stood alone on the back of my sled with my dogs pulling wildly as the other teams prepared to go. He had also mentioned something about the foot brake not holding in soft snow. My hands tightened into a death grip on the handlebar as it became all too clear that I was taking off alone on a vehicle with a throttle stuck wide open, no steering wheel, and brakes that had already failed to hold at a stop. The parking brake—a grappling hook optimistically kicked into soft snow—pulled out from the jerks of the dogs, and we were off like a runaway truck.

After the first mile, the dogs became easy to stop after they'd run enough to get hot and tired. As I gained control of my team, my grip on the handlebar eased enough to hold on with one hand and take pictures of my team heading into the Brooks Range, using my strategically placed shadow to hint at my presence. *(Nikon N90, 35–70mm f2.8 lens, f5.6 at 1/250 second, Fuji Velvia)*

Northern lights over Mount Gilroy, Brooks Range, Alaska; 1994 *p. 91*

On our first day out from Bettles, five-and-a-half hours of mellow mushing through rolling boreal forest brought us 26 miles to an exquisite campsite beneath Mount Gilroy. We were near the edge of Gates of the Arctic National Park and Preserve, which we would enter the next morning. Everyone pitched in to feed and care for the dogs and set up the tents. When we came out after dinner, an eerie green banner of northern lights was dancing across the starry sky. I set up my camera on a tripod and began shooting dozens of 30-second exposures to get one that held the best definition. A clear night in the Brooks Range is not something to be taken for granted. It proved to be the only fine display of the aurora borealis that we saw during a week on the trail. *(Nikon N90, 35mm f1.4 lens, f5.6 at 30 seconds, Fuji Velvia)*

Sled dog sleeping outside in winter in Gates of the Arctic National Park, Brooks Range, Alaska; 1994 *p. 91*

Dogs running on a winter trail are as thoroughly happy as any creatures I have ever seen, including humans on tropical beaches. Their comfort range seems similar. Until it gets around -30°F, many sled dogs don't bother to sleep inside their kennels. During rest stops on the trail, they roll in the snow to cool off, just like a hot beached human dipping in the surf.

Some people believe sleds dogs are mistreated because they have to pull sleds for long hours and sleep chained up out in the cold. At first, I expected my dogs to try to break free when I harnessed them each morning, but they were far more interested in being hooked up to pull with their buddies than in going off by themselves. I doubt the contented dog I photographed curled up with a dusting of snow on a -5°F morning would trade places with any of his kind who live in Manhattan apartments.

I got to know each member of my team by name and personality. Friday and Cocoa were my lead dogs. Digger and Fax were my wheel dogs, the pair just in front of the sled that do the hardest pulling. In the middle were Sam and Moe, a pair of bad actors who provided most of the entertainment as well as the problems. Whenever a fight began, Moe was always the instigator and Sam was always the whiner, rolling over on the ground in such an exaggerated display of submission that even I was tempted to bite him. *(Nikon F4, 35–70mm f2.8 lens, f16 at 1/4 second, Fuji Velvia)*

Galen Rowell running a dog team in Gates of the Arctic National Park, Brooks Range, Alaska; 1994 (photograph by Bill Mackey) *p. 91*

On a windless morning under a cloudy sky we headed up Michigan Creek into the valley of the Koyukuk toward the Gates of the Arctic: two peaks named Boreal Mountain and Frigid Crags by the explorer Robert Marshall in the thirties. After the dogs began to seriously tire in the deep, soft snow, Bill Mackey, our guide, called it a day after only four hours. We dropped our gear at a campsite and continued on unladen for a good view of the Gates. After I asked Bill to run his team past me several times for photos, he volunteered to take a picture of me with my camera that the two of us set up before I crested a nearby hill. *(Nikon F4, 85mm f2 lens, f2.8 at 1/500 second, Fuji Velvia)*

Approaching Cape Crozier in a blizzard, Ross Island, Antarctica; 1992 *p. 92*

I took this photograph on my second attempt to reach Cape Crozier in the early spring with Dr. Gerald Kooyman of Scripps Institution of Oceanography and his team of emperor penguin researchers. On our first try we drove snowmobiles 45 miles into a zone of crevassed sea ice at the edge of the Ross Ice Shelf, then scrambled with crampons for several hours without reaching the penguin colony. A ground blizzard set in, and we set up tents about 3 miles from the colony. After waiting out the windstorm for several days, we managed to break camp and return to McMurdo Station. On our next attempt a week later, we drove tracked vehicles high onto the slopes of the island just before entering the crevasse field. When we could take them no farther across the windblown rocks, we set up camp about 1,000 feet above and 2 miles away from the colony on a perfect windless night. In the morning, a 50-knot wind was blowing and the visibility was less than 10 feet. I expected us to be pinned down for days, but when the winds dropped to about 40 knots in the early afternoon, Jerry suggested that we give it a try. I used a medium telephoto to freeze him midstep as he led us through a blizzard to the colony out on the sea ice, where the winds eased considerably and we spent a splendid afternoon. *(Nikon N90, 85mm f2 lens, f4 at 1/250 second, Fuji Velvia)*

Dr. Gerald Kooyman reading from *The Worst Journey in the World*, **Cape Crozier, Ross Island, Antarctica; 1992** *p. 92*

At several points along the way to Cape Crozier, Jerry Kooyman took out a copy of Apsley Cherry-Gerrard's superb book and read aloud descriptive passages about his epic 1911 winter journey with two companions. Here, we were gathered around the remains of the *Worst Journey's* igloo at Cape Crozier, where the three men had barely survived a blizzard that blew their canvas tarp away. Cherry-Gerrard wrote of their suffering: "We on this journey were already beginning to think of death as a friend." Before us were a circle of rocks, several freeze-dried emperor penguin carcasses, a box of provisions, plus tattered scraps of rope, clothing, and the still-greenish Willesden canvas from their roof. When Jerry finished reading, all six of us signed his book at this designated Antarctic Treaty historic site. *(Nikon N90, 35–70mm f2.8 lens, f5.6 at 1/125 second, Fuji Velvia)*

Emperor penguins at Cape Crozier, Ross Island, Antarctica; 1992 *p. 93*

When we finally arrived at the Cape Crozier colony, I was somewhat disappointed that the 500 emperor penguins were quite dirty from spending weeks together in the heart of the colony with their chicks. We expect sentient beings in tuxedos to have a clean appearance. In photographs, scruffy emperor penguins call attention to their untidiness in a way that dirty blue-collar birds, such as hawks or skuas, do not. Adding to my photographic difficulties, Jerry Kooyman reminded me that we were in a "Specially Protected Area" of the Antarctic Treaty by permit for scientific purposes only. He said not to approach the penguins closer than 200 feet. However, if I stayed still and the penguins approached me, the encounter would be on their terms and perfectly okay. On our way to the colony on the second morning, this group of emperors emerged sparkling clean from a distant hole in the ice. They had gone out to sea to fill their bellies with squid and fish to feed their chicks. I stayed put, and they slowly wandered over to check me out. As the first rays of the sun crept over the heights of Ross Island, I snapped this image looking down at them with a wide-angle lens. Moments later, the lead penguin pecked my tripod and headed off toward the colony, with the others following behind in single file. *(Nikon F4, 24mm f2.8 lens, f11 at 1/30 second, Fuji Velvia)*

Dr. Gerald Kooyman photographing an emperor penguin, Cape Crozier, Ross Island, Antarctica; 1992 *p. 93*
When I saw this scene out of the corner of my eye, I stopped photographing another penguin to capture the essence of what I myself had just been doing. I carefully thought about how to compose the picture. I did not want to place the bird and the man equidistant from the center of the image, because that would imply an equality that I did not believe existed. I purposely positioned Jerry at the edge of the frame—a temporary visitor to the realm where the birds live year round. I spaced the penguin farther into the frame, but not so far that the area behind it drew attention by exceeding the distance between it and Jerry. The emphasis needed to be clearly focused on this curious meeting of individuals of very different species. *(Nikon F4, 80–200mm f2.8 lens, f8 at 1/250 second, Fuji Velvia)*

Emperor penguin with telemetry device, Cape Crozier, Ross Island, Antarctica; 1992 *p. 93*

After Jerry Kooyman's team attached a radio transmitter to an emperor's back with epoxy glue, it waddled back to its mate as if nothing had happened. Within a month or so, the device would fall off after delivering via satellite to a receiving station in the United States information on the bird's travels. Times have changed, though the human mission has not, since Cherry-Gerrard closed *The Worst Journey in the World* about his 1911 trip to Cape Crozier with these words: "If you have the desire for knowledge and the power to give it physical expression, go out and explore. . . . Some will tell you that you are mad, and nearly all will say, 'What is the use?' For we are a nation of shopkeepers, and no shopkeeper will look at research which does not promise him a financial return within a year. And so you will sledge nearly alone, but those with whom you sledge will not be shopkeepers: that is worth a good deal. If you march your Winter Journeys you will have your reward, so long as all you want is a penguin's egg." *(Nikon F4, 80–200mm f2.8 lens, f5.6 at 1/250 second, Fuji Velvia)*

Ice scientist sawing slabs of sea ice on a -32°F morning, Point Barrow, Alaska; 1994 *p. 94*
While on a winter visit to Barrow I got up early each morning and drove miles out of town to look for polar bears or interplays of light upon the landscape. One day I spotted figures several miles away out on the sea ice beside a tent. I was surprised to find a crew working outside cutting blocks out of the 5-foot-thick ice with a giant saw. They turned out to be scientists from the University of Alaska and the local Ukpeagvik Inupiat Corporation, who were doing large-scale ice fracture experiments to more accurately predict the safety of offshore structures on sea ice. People used to believe that crushing was the usual cause of sea-ice failure, but sideways splitting at much lower loads is by far more common.

Scientists now know that resistance to splitting varies with direction in relation to the internal structure of the ice and how it formed. Test-loading full-scale blocks in the field gave these researchers far better data than simulated laboratory tests. *(Nikon F4, 35–70mm f2.8 lens, SB-25 flash, f5.6 at 1/125 second, Fuji Velvia)*

Jennelle Marcereau working in portable lab, Toolik Field Station, Brooks Range, Alaska; 1993 *p. 95*
Arctic field science has no dedicated research facilities that come even close to those in the Antarctic, where logistical support from the National Science Foundation makes research possible in the total absence of permanent residents. Beyond the Arctic Circle in the United States, a small cluster of trailers and temporary buildings beside a lake on the North Slope of the Brooks Range is the nearest analog to the huge Antarctic science complex at McMurdo Station. The Toolik Field Station is operated by the University of Alaska, although researchers from many institutions conduct studies there. Here, Jennelle Marcereau is doing research for the national Marine Biological Laboratory at Woods Hole, Massachusetts, as part of the Long-Term Ecological Research Program with funding from the National Science Foundation. She is measuring changes in nutrient fluxes from land to water systems to better understand the buffering capacity of tundra groundwater against acid rain and other aspects of climate change. The answers are not simple or easily predictable. Rock, soil, flora, and fauna all have a role in controlling the highly variable chemistry of the water that flows over Arctic landscapes. I used an off-camera flash mounted in a portable soft box to supply even fill light to balance with the scene out the window. *(Nikon F4, 20mm f2.8 lens, SB-25 flash, f8 at 1/30 second, Fuji Velvia)*

Full moon over rocket launcher, Churchill Research Range, Manitoba; 1993 *p. 95*
As I walked out of the Churchill Northern Studies Center at dawn to take off for the day in a helicopter with polar bear biologists, I noticed a full moon setting near the horizon. I circled the nearby launch tower of the inactive Churchill Research Range until I could position the moon within the tilt of the structure and use a telephoto lens on a tripod. Beginning at the time of the International Geophysical Year in 1957–58, unguided Aerobee rockets with scientific payloads were sent hundreds of miles into the upper atmosphere to study northern lights, Arctic haze, and other chemical components of the atmosphere, such as ozone levels. Flights continued until 1989, when political and budgetary problems caused their termination. Plans are under way to resume them. *(Nikon F4, 80–200mm f2.8 lens, f5.6 at 1/60 second, Fuji Velvia)*

Crary Laboratory and Royal Society Range, McMurdo Station, Antarctica; 1992 *p. 96*
Two days after the beginning of 24-hour daylight in October, I stayed out all night around McMurdo to photograph in continuous hours of sunset light as the sun moved horizontally just above the crest of the Royal Society Range of the Transantarctic Mountains. Just after three in the morning, a warm glow struck the metal walls and rooftop paraphernalia of the

brand-new lab officially called the Alfred P. Crary Science and Engineering Center. I set up an extreme telephoto on a tripod to single out the high-tech building from its undistinguished neighbors, as well as to pull the distant Royal Society Range much closer. The $25 million lab was in its first season of full operation with state-of-the-art computer work stations, cold labs, library and lecture room, and much more. What impressed me most was that top scientists of very different disciplines were brought together under the same roof where they socialized and cross-pollinated one another's ideas, instead of working in ivory towers. *(Nikon F4, 300mm f2.8 lens, f16 at 1/4 second, Fuji Velvia)*

Dr. Sean Turner culturing algae in a cold lab, Crary Laboratory, McMurdo Station, Antarctica; 1992 *p. 96*
After a season of storage in a low-temperature incubator at -80°C (-112°F), a sample of algae from permanently ice-covered Lake Hoare in the Dry Valleys blooms with life. Agitation and oxygenation at temperatures a little above freezing rapidly cultured the algae in a laboratory analog of Antarctic summer—the banana belt for an Antarctic plant that evolved in the cold. Other samples have been cultured from crypto-endolithic algae that grow just below the surface of the sandstones of the Dry Valleys and from old ice taken from stable ice shelf sites. The purpose of the experiments is to study the molecular mechanisms that enable biotic systems to adapt to extreme cold and ascertain their evolutionary relationship to species in temperate latitudes.

I made this photograph on a high tripod with a very wide lens pointed downward. A portable Photoflex soft box supplied the warm, even light on the foreground, while the fluorescent lighting of the lab is rendered greenish on daylight film. *(Nikon F4, 20mm f2.8 lens, SB-25 flash, f16 at 1 second, Fuji Velvia)*

Dr. Charles Knight studying ice crystals in a cold lab, Crary Laboratory, McMurdo Station, Antarctica; 1992 *p. 97*
In the foreground of this photograph is an "optic axis interference figure," commonly called a cross, in a polarized section of a large single ice crystal grown in the Crary Laboratory. By using an extremely wide 15mm rectilinear lens, I was able to hold the cross and interference fringes in sharp focus and at the same time show Dr. Charles Knight, lit by a portable Photoflex soft box, examining a similar crystal section under the microscope. He wears a heavy parka in a cold room kept near 0°F to preserve the crystals. The research, led for the past thirty years by Dr. Arthur DeVries, is part of an ongoing study of the creation and functioning of antifreeze proteins in Antarctic fish. DeVries sees broad implications of this work for such fields as human physiology, nucleation theory, and crystallography. Fish wouldn't survive in the southern oceans without some way to prevent the freezing of body fluids in saltwater that is several degrees below 32°F. The chemicals we add to our cars actually lower the freezing point of water, whereas fish "antifreeze" works very differently by blocking crystallization with no change in the true freezing point. *(Nikon F4, 15mm f3.5 lens, SB-25 flash, f16 at 1/2 second, Fuji Velvia)*

Rod Rozier releasing ozone balloon at McMurdo Station, Antarctica; 1992 *p. 97*

Behind this simple image of a scientist releasing a balloon to measure ozone levels is one of the most publicly debated and thoroughly misunderstood issues of our time. After spending time with scientists doing ozone research at McMurdo and the South Pole, I realized that they disagree with media accounts of many basic "facts." Chlorofluorocarbons (CFCs) do not directly deplete ozone over America, and are not part of strong natural fluctuations that preexisted the CFC-enhanced "hole" recently discovered over Antarctica, yet they are a major cause for global concern.

I used fill-flash to isolate this balloon against the clouds as it began to lift an aerosol counter 20 miles up and 120 miles out onto the Ross Ice Shelf, where a satellite beacon guided a helicopter recovery that I also photographed. On October 9, the day before I arrived in McMurdo, a balloon released by this University of Wyoming team had measured record ozone depletion of 84 percent in the lower stratosphere. A narrower zone of near-total depletion coincided with an observed aerosol layer of sulfuric acid droplets from the 1991 eruption of Mount Pinatubo. The scientists reported this along with other "evidence that ozone depletion over Antarctica is significantly enhanced by the presence of volcanic aerosol." They made no rush to judgment that ozone depletion is wholly natural, unlike the aptly named talk-show host, "Rush" Limbaugh, whose enormous popularity at the time of this writing stems from playing into public apathy over the most complex global problems by setting minds at ease with a simplistic gospel of slick answers. On the other side of the issue, *Time* magazine's off-target reporting is laced with anecdotal hysteria, such as tales of ozone-blinded Patagonian sheep.

Atmospheric scientists agree that artificial CFCs entering the naturally unstable conditions that exist over Antarctica each spring create or augment the seasonal appearance of an ozone "hole" that can be as big as the United States—an event unlikely to occur in the temperate latitudes, although a slower, cumulative ozone loss is likely enough to be a matter of scientific debate. In the atmosphere as we know it today, the observed reaction that causes a massive ozone hole is unique to special circumstances in Antarctica. Polar stratospheric clouds must breed the proper chemistry during months of winter darkness

without escaping the polar vortex into sunlight (as they do in the Arctic). Extreme stratospheric temperatures that may reach -130°F must persist into the Antarctic spring (which has been colder in recent years for unknown reasons). Only then can energy from sunlight combine with highly reactive chlorine compounds, which otherwise could not exist in the ozone layer, to set off a catalytic reaction comparable to a chain letter. One chlorine monoxide molecule can destroy thousands of ozone molecules. *(Nikon N90, 28–70mm f3.5 lens, SB-25 flash, f4 at 1/125 second, Fuji Velvia)*

Inupiat Eskimo whaling captain in umiak beside an open lead in the Arctic Ocean, near Barrow, Alaska; 1994 *p. 98*
I camped for a week beside this open lead with a whaling crew of five Inupiat Eskimos. Sometimes winds and currents would almost close the lead, while at others it would spread open to more than a mile across, as it is here, without a ripple, on a rare still evening. At least one of us kept watch twenty-four hours a day for whales, bears, or dangerous movement of the sea ice. In this scene Thomas Brower III, our captain, is in the bow of his umiak at the ready. While I slept in a sleeping bag in my own tent, the Eskimos remained fully clothed and ready to be up at a moment's notice in a canvas wall tent that was kept near room temperature with a propane heater. Someone always had a hand on a loaded rifle in case of polar bears. Past generations of subsistence whalers slept equally ready in the cold in full suits of caribou fur. *(Nikon F4, 24mm f2.8 lens, f16 at 1/2 second, Fuji Velvia)*

Bowhead whale breaching in open lead in the Arctic Ocean, near Barrow, Alaska; 1994 *p. 99*

During the first few days I camped beside this open lead with an Eskimo whaling crew, the whales I saw were all far away. I set up a tripod with a special fourth leg to support a 500mm lens with two tele-converters stacked to obtain 1420mm of magnification. I felt quite satisfied after catching this breach at a distance of a mile. (Note how close the far side of the lead appears from the same camera position as in the previous image.) I was using the same lens when our crew pushed off after a whale far out in the lead. Then, entirely without warning, a bowhead did a full breach in front of me, 30 feet off shore. The huge lens was useless, as was the telephoto zoom on my other camera. I turned my head upward as the animal leapt into the sky, and quickly stepped back to avoid the big wave that splashed onto the ice. For a moment I was disappointed not to have caught the breach on film, but then came the inner glow of having witnessed one of the most powerful wildlife sightings of my life. I spent the rest of the week with an autofocus point-and-shoot around my neck, but never saw anything like this breach again. *(Nikon F4, 500mm f4 lens with 2X and 1.4X teleconverters, f4 at 1/250 second, Kodak Lumiere 100 push processed to ISO 200)*

Sunset after an Inupiat Eskimo whale hunt near Barrow, Alaska; 1994 *p. 99*

The ancestors of the modern Inupiat Eskimos of the Arctic coast were actively hunting bowhead whales over 1,000 years ago. They had developed their own equipment and had studied the annual migration to determine the best sites for hunting. The flip side of living in a permafrost area is year-round free cold storage of meat, which would otherwise spoil, in ice cellars dug into the ground. Here, an Inupiat Eskimo watches the sunset over the pack ice a few hours after a successful whale hunt. I used a wide-angle lens on a tripod with a Singh-Ray three-stop graduated neutral-density filter to balance detail on the snow against the drama of the sky.

Villagers who had come out from Barrow to help land and butcher the whale returned home with chunks of meat and blubber. Except for the skeleton, the whale was virtually gone by the next morning. *(Nikon F4, 20mm f4 lens, f16 at 1 second, Fuji Velvia)*

Inupiat Eskimos landing a bowhead whale onto the pack ice of the Arctic Ocean, near Barrow, Alaska; 1994 *p. 99*

After Thomas Brower III harpooned a whale right in front of me (see page 70), he announced the kill over his radio. Within the hour, villagers arrived by snowmobile to help winch the 33.5-foot leviathan onto the ice and butcher it for distribution throughout the village. I used a 16mm extremely wide-angle lens to take in the scene, centering the horizon to keep it from curving.

The following day, friends poured into Thomas's home in Barrow for an informal banquet of whale delicacies. It became very

clear why coastal Eskimos say that subsistence whaling is the glue that holds their remaining traditional culture together. I thought about the moment of triumph of the previous day's hunt, and how skills passed down from father to son for generations had come together for Thomas out on the ice in a way bearing no resemblance to the career moves urbanites take so seriously. Visitors who see Barrow on one-day tours often find the place bleak and can't imagine why anyone would live there. Three of the five Eskimos of Thomas's crew had returned to Barrow after years at school in bigger cities. After the hunt, I wrote in my journal: "The Arctic gives you back what you put into it. If you always keep searching for a warm fire or a place out of the wind, you may stay in a tent, create a town, or continue searching, unsatisfied. But if you accept it for what it is and work within its limitations, you discover another world. You understand why Eskimos who have tried moving to Seattle or Anchorage suddenly pack up and return to Barrow with a passion." *(Nikon F4, 16mm f2.8 lens, f5.6 at 1/60 second, Fuji Velvia)*

Science lab in Scott's Hut, Cape Evans, Ross Island, Antarctica; 1992 *p. 100*

I originally conceived this image for a picture story on the history of Antarctic science, but for this book's brief spreads on discrete subjects, the image fit better with historic huts. I used a wide-angle lens and subtle fill-flash to light the deep shadows on the left, while holding an exposure for the natural light coming through the window onto the right of the desk. Scott never returned to this hut after his tragic trip to the pole. After it was last used by the Ross Sea members of Shackleton's 1914–17 expedition, it filled with snow over the years. Not until 1960, as the Antarctic Treaty was about to go into effect, was the hut cleaned out by a New Zealand committee and locked for controlled visitation. Every attempt was made to keep items where Scott's

men had left them. Few labels survived, but many of the bottles still hold their original chemicals. In the same hut is photographer Herbert Ponting's darkroom, with all its original chemistry and paraphernalia. *(Nikon F4, 20mm f4 lens, SB-25 flash, f16 at 1 second, Fuji Velvia)*

Scott's Hut in a blizzard, Cape Evans, Ross Island, Antarctica; 1992 *p. 100*

Captain Robert Falcon Scott built this hut in January 1911 as a base for his attempt to reach the South Pole after wintering over. It sits 17 miles from his original 1902 "Discovery" hut beside the present site of the U.S. McMurdo Station. I first visited this hut when it was partly blown over with snow in the early spring. After we dug out the door and stepped inside, I was surprised by its great size and relative comfort. The 50-by-25-foot building even has a stable for the ill-fated ponies Scott tried to use instead of dogs. As I left in high winds, I looked back and saw a scene that emphasized the hut's wild and remote setting. I stopped and made this shot with a long telephoto lens braced on the roof of the tracked vehicle I was driving. *(Nikon F4, 300mm f2.8 lens, f5.6 at 1/30 second, Fuji Velvia)*

Emperor penguin carcass in Scott's Hut, Cape Evans, Antarctica; 1992 *p. 101*

The origin of this emperor penguin sitting on a desk in Dr. Edward Wilson's corner of Scott's Hut is uncertain. Wilson was the driving force behind "the worst journey in the world" to Cape Crozier (see pages 92–93). There he collected emperor eggs to be examined in Britain by scientists to see if their embryonic development would confirm them as a missing link to reptiles. He also collected several adult emperor specimens. This may have been one of them, although no specific mention of it being left in Scott's Hut is made in Cherry-Gerrard's long book. The colors of its feathers remain as vivid as those of a live penguin. After my visit to the hut, I wrote in my journal, "The carcass of an emperor penguin looks like it was cured for a museum just yesterday, but I think it is a naturally freeze-dried specimen, brought in from the wild as-is." I made the photograph with a wide-angle lens on a low tripod, using a combination of warm evening light coming in through a window and fill light from a portable soft box filtered to match the natural light as closely as possible. *(Nikon F4, 24mm f2.8 lens, SB-25 flash, f11 at 1/4 second, Fuji Velvia)*

Newspaper in Shackleton's Hut, Cape Royds, Antarctica; 1992 *p. 101*
Among the incredibly well preserved items inside Shackleton's 1908 hut is an undated part of a newspaper with travel advertisements from the period of his expedition. I can imagine his men poring over dream journeys to warm beaches as they waited out an Antarctic winter to attempt the pole in the fierce cold of the early spring. The paper shows no noticeable yellowing after spending most of a century in a dark building well below freezing—a metaphor for the nonbiodegradable nature of most anything left behind in the Antarctic. Cape Royds is 8 miles from Cape Evans, where Scott built a hut three years after Shackleton built this one, on a site that was not his first choice. Heavy sea ice prevented Shackleton's ship from reaching Winter Quarters Bay, the present site of McMurdo Station, where he had previously wintered with Scott's 1902 expedition. *(Nikon F4, 55mm f2.8 lens, f16 at 1/2 second, Fuji Velvia)*

Provisions in Shackleton's Hut, Cape Royds, Antarctica; 1992 *p. 101*
Most of the labels on jars and cans that remain on the shelves of Shackleton's 1908 hut are clear and readable. Dark contents inside the glass jars appeared to bear little relationship to the names on the labels or the colors I expected to see. The snow on top of the lids is spindrift driven through cracks by winter blizzards. I used a portable Photoflex soft box to bathe the shelf in the kind of warm light that would have come from an explorer's oil lamp or fire.

We were the first visitors of the season in the early spring. The hut seemed bleak as we dug several feet of snow away from the door, but I could imagine how cozy and warm it would have seemed to Shackleton's team, when it was in daily use with tons of coal, food, and special equipment brought by ship. Above the entrance to the 23-by-19-foot building is a quite sophisticated boiler for running hot water. Outside are parts of the first automobile in Antarctica, a 15-horsepower Arrol-Johnston that Shackleton used with even less success than Scott had with his poor ponies. *(Nikon F4, 55mm f2.8 lens, SB-25 flash, f11 at 1/2 second, Fuji Velvia)*

Traversing the Peters Glacier below Mount McKinley (20,320 feet), Denali National Park, Alaska; 1978 *p. 102*
When I circled Mount McKinley with a bush pilot in 1972, I was amazed by the interconnecting pattern of five major glaciers, each one longer than any in the Nepal Himalaya, that flow down the peak and abruptly turn to form a ring of ice 90 miles in circumference. Because of its location in the subpolar latitudes, McKinley's great circle of moving ice, entirely above timberline in uninhabited wilderness, is unique among the 20,000-foot peaks of the world. On the first traverse of this route in 1978, my team of four encountered wild Arctic conditions on the Peters Glacier. A ground blizzard driven by high winds off the mountain transformed the glacier's surface into a mystical frozen ocean of icy waves and swells. Minutes after I took this telephoto, Alan Bard was blown over with a 90-pound pack and dislocated his shoulder. He skied into camp that day with his arm held helplessly against his chest, but spent two more weeks completing the journey. Though we crossed the three main buttresses of the peak at altitudes of up to 13,000 feet, our journey lacked the geographical climax of a summit. We knew we had reached completion when we found our own windblown tracks from nineteen days before. *(Nikon FM, 200mm f4 lens, f5.6 at 1/250 second, Kodachrome 25)*

Sunrise on Mount McKinley (20,320 feet), Denali National Park, Alaska; 1991 *p. 102*
The north side of Mount McKinley has the greatest vertical rise in North America—17,500 feet above the rolling hills of Denali National Park. This long telephoto was made in extremely clear air just after an October snowstorm. On the right is the lower north peak, climbed by mistake in 1910 by a pair of sourdoughs who planted a 14-foot spruce flagpole at the end of an amazing 8,500-foot one-day climb from 10,800 feet. In 1978, when Ned Gillette and I conceived the idea of climbing the main peak in a single day from Kahiltna Pass at 10,000 feet, the fastest ascent to date had been done in three days. Most climbers take two to four weeks. They move at a snail's pace, because like that mollusk, they must carry their homes on their backs. Our goal was not a speed record, but the experience of climbing the wild environment of the upper mountain unencumbered by huge amounts of gear, as the sourdoughs had done long before on the north peak. *(Nikon F4, 300mm f2.8 lens, f4 at 1/125 second, Fuji Velvia)*

Ned Gillette at 16,000 feet on first one-day ascent of Mount McKinley (20,320 feet), Denali National Park, Alaska; 1978 *p. 102*
Three nights after coming up from sea level to a camp at 10,000-foot Kahiltna Pass below Mount McKinley, Ned Gillette and I started out for the summit in perfect weather with light 17-pound packs. In mid-June the sun shone for 24 hours on the summit ramparts, but set for a few hours lower down without the night ever becoming dark. After we reached 18,200-foot Denali Pass in the early morning, it took many more hours to lug our tired, unacclimatized bodies to the top. We descended back to 17,000 feet, where we rested for a few hours before continuing down to the skis we had cached below. I made this photograph with a tiny 6.6-ounce Minox, which froze up and broke a shutter in the -20°F conditions near the top. Since then, I have always used full-size Nikon SLR cameras in extreme cold without a single cold-related problem that couldn't be solved with either new or remotely attached batteries. *(Minox 35 EL, 40mm f3.5 lens, f3.5 at 1/30 second, Kodachrome 64)*

Alpenglow on corniced ridge, Mount McKinley (20,320 feet), Denali National Park, Alaska; 1979 *p. 103*

The year after I made a one-day ascent of Mount McKinley, *National Geographic* hired me to photograph a three-week traverse of the peak for a book, *America's Magnificent Mountains*. I joined a guided expedition with a *Geographic* writer and six other clients that gave me a great opportunity to make images of light and form I had seen on my one-day climb but had been unable to photograph properly with my tiny Minox 35 EL. I remembered seeing fantastic light in the wee hours of the morning on a corniced ridge at the top of a steep headwall that topped out at 16,000 feet. When our expedition camped just above the ridge, I ventured out shortly before midnight in -22°F temperatures to capture the edge of last light, which emphasized the form of a convoluted cornice by casting a pink glow on one side against deep blue shadows on the other. *(Nikon FM, 200mm f4 lens, f16 at 1/2 second, Kodachrome 25)*

Ned Gillette skiing down Mount McKinley (20,320 feet) after first one-day ascent, Alaska; 1978 *p. 103*

Ned and I used short mountaineering skis with climbing skins for the first 3,500 feet of our one-day ascent of Mount McKinley. We cached them on our way up and finished our round-trip with a superb downhill run through icefalls and snow bowls,

164

passing crevasses at points we had carefully checked out during our ascent. This photograph was handheld with a short telephoto at a place where I asked Ned to stop and ski by me. I had also cached my Nikon FM with my skis, a decision I now regret, because the tiny Minox I took higher failed me. I had been trying to follow the minutely detailed sort of preplanning that had given my friend Reinhold Messner success on Alpine-style ascents in the Himalaya, where he contemplated "not one match too many, nor one match too few." During the same season we were on this climb, Reinhold Messner and Peter Habeler were making the first climb of Mount Everest without oxygen. *(Nikon FM, 105mm f2.8 lens, f4 at 1/500 second, Kodachrome 25)*

Ice cave below Mount Erebus (12,447 feet), Ross Island, Antarctica; 1992 *p. 104*

One evening in October, I visited a remote camp about 10 miles from McMurdo Station where researchers from the University of Alaska were studying Weddell seals. After I had witnessed the birth of a seal (see page 45), Steve Lewis joined me on cross-country skis to explore some large icebergs trapped in the sea ice. I spotted an ice cave about 50 feet up the face of one berg and scouted it for a photograph. With my back against the inside wall, I could frame Mount Erebus in warm evening light through a blue-shadowed diagonal hole. I put a Singh-Ray two-stop graduated neutral-density filter on a wide-angle lens to open up detail in the foreground and asked Steve to stand in the cave's mouth with ice ax in hand looking up and left into the visual flow of my composition. Mount Erebus is less known to the public for its beauty than for the 1979 disaster in which a low-flying Air New Zealand DC-10 sightseeing flight with an error programmed into its flight computer hit the lower slopes of the peak, killing all 257 persons aboard. *(Nikon N90, 28–70mm f3.5 lens, f11 at 1/30 second, Fuji Velvia)*

Crater rim of Mount Erebus (12,447 feet), Ross Island, Antarctica; 1992 *p. 104*

During an entire night spent walking around the crater rim of this active volcano, I decided to make a photograph that would capture the scale of the place. I used a 16mm ultra-wide lens to show the whole crater with my companion positioned on the rim at the upper right. A 1978 attempt to reach the bottom failed when a minor eruption pelted a scientist, who was being lowered into the inner crater, with molten volcanic bombs, searing his insulated clothing. The scientist barely escaped with his life. Since 1983, the National Science Foundation has frowned on manned missions into the crater, but it recently supported a project by Carnegie-Mellon Institute to send a robot named Dante to the bottom of the crater to gather gas and rock samples. I planned to be on the summit in November 1992 to photograph Dante, but the robot broke its legs during a test run on a Pittsburgh slag heap. After several weeks' delay, the Mount Erebus experiment ended prematurely when Dante severed his fiber-optic control cable just 6 feet below the rim on the way down. *(Nikon F4, 16mm f2.8 lens, f5.6 at 1/125 second, Fuji Velvia)*

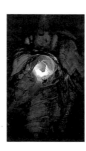

Ice cave near crater rim of Mount Erebus (12,447 feet), Ross Island, Antarctica; 1992 *p. 105*

Before heading off for Mount Erebus, Tim Cully and I talked with Bill McIntosh, an adventurous geologist who had lived on the side of the active volcano for months at a time over a period of years to study its explosive habits. After drawing maps of where to go and what to see, he suggested that if we ever got bored, we could drop into "Mammoth Cave" from a hole at the top of one of the smaller ice towers near the crater rim. He assured us that the size of the ice crystals in large subterranean chambers beneath the tower were not only worth the effort to see, but also evidence of relatively stable conditions in recent years. On our third afternoon, I crawled out onto thin ice over the steaming hole but couldn't see if my doubled 165-foot rope would reach the bottom. I reset the rappel to go down on a single strand and slowly eased into the misty black void anchored to Jumar ascenders as a backup in case part of the 10-foot cornice broke. When I touched the level floor of dark pumice, I told Tim to wait until I was ready for a photograph. I quickly set my Nikon N90 with a manual exposure for the blue sky. I used an on-camera SB-25 flash unit set at a -1.7 exposure compensation with a 70mm zoom head adjustment to project a narrowed beam of perfectly balanced light that would not cause overly bright reflections off the closer walls of the cave. *(Nikon N90, 24mm f2.8 lens, SB-25 flash, f5.6 at 1/250 second, Fuji Velvia)*

Windblown *sastrugi* on the upper slopes of Mount Erebus (12,447 feet), Ross Island, Antarctica; 1992 *p. 105*

While walking across rock-hard, wind-polished *sastrugi* near the top of Mount Erebus, I noticed how it reflected the warm sunlight of a spring evening. *Sastrugi* is a Russian word now used in many languages to describe exposed ice and snow eroded into convoluted patterns by strong unidirectional winds. I tried to imagine my ideal photograph of this light and form coming together and how to make it happen. Flat slopes wouldn't do, so I sought out the curving crest of a ridge that rolled away from the camera and dropped off suddenly to expose a distant horizon. In the very bright light, I was able to handhold a wide-angle lens at a small aperture to hold maximum depth of field. *(Nikon N90, 24mm f2.8 lens, f22 at 1/60 second, Fuji Velvia)*

Ice tower on Mount Erebus, Ross Island, Antarctica; 1992 *p. 105*

This is one of the group of hollow ice towers formed around steam fumaroles shown in the photograph on page 87. Steam is breaching through a hole in the side of this "Leaning Tower of Erebus," which appeared ready to topple. Eruptions are of even more concern to explorers of these towers. Both of the first two teams to climb the peak early in the century experienced violent eruptions and managed to escape. In recent years the mountain has been somewhat more quiet, although hundreds of minor eruptions occur each year. I breathed a sigh of relief when, after spending several hours in a cave, I surfaced and saw the mountain looking unchanged. *(Nikon n90, 20mm f4 lens, f8 at 1/30 second, Fuji Velvia)*

Polar bear cub resting against its mother, Cape Churchill, Manitoba, Canada; 1993 *p. 106*

I had a remarkable opportunity to photograph a second-year cub in the wild at close range after it charged a researcher who had just tranquilized its mother from a helicopter (a process also described in the next two essays). Normal procedure is to use a dart rifle from the air only on the mother. As cubs cling naturally to their mother's

side, they are tranquilized on the ground by researchers who approach with a long probe to hand-inject a few drops of Telazol, a carnivore wonder drug used by my friend George Schaller to tranquilize precious pandas in Asia before it was tried on polar bears. The procedure is more reliable on a 20-pound cub-of-the-year than a 250-pound, two-year-old carnivore on the verge of being weaned after its litter mate is already gone.

As the team of five performed physiological tests on the mother, I was captivated by the cub, who kept lifting its head and staring at me. The researchers assured me that this was normal behavior and that the cub could not otherwise move. I later read that native hunters working with biologists had been spooked by the apparent full awareness of polar bears on Telazol. I moved in close with a normal lens on a tripod and shot an entire roll at a small aperture that would hold full sharpness from the cub's huge paw to the mother's back. Suddenly the cub raised up on its front legs and faced me. I took a giant step backward as the researchers gave it another Telazol shot. *(Nikon N90, 35–70mm f2.8 lens, SB-25 flash, f16 at 1/15 second, Fuji Velvia)*

Polar bear cub charging researcher, Cape Churchill, Manitoba, Canada; 1993 *p. 107*

In Steve Miller's Jet Ranger helicopter, six of us followed a signal from a radio collar on a mother bear. After we tranquilized her from the helicopter with a rifle dart, we landed and slowly approached the mother bear with her large cub curled up beside her. Susan Polischuk, a graduate student of Dr. Malcolm Ramsey at the University of Saskatchewan, carried a probe to inject the cub with Telazol. As I watched through my viewfinder, the cub suddenly charged past the probe and stopped a foot short of mauling Polischuk. I would like to have seen *her* pulse and respiration monitored at the time.

She kept her cool and succeeded in darting the cub on her second try as an assistant covered her with a 44 Magnum. The cub's charge that stopped short must have been a bluff, never intended as a full-on attack, for, as the esteemed polar bear expert Ian Stirling says, "A polar bear attack on a human ends only when one of them is dead." *(Nikon N90, 35–70mm f2.8 lens, f5.6 at 1/250 second, Fuji Velvia)*

Biologists studying tranquilized polar bears, Cape Churchill, Manitoba, Canada; 1993 *p. 107*

After tranquilizing the mother and cub described in the previous essays, Susan Polischuk and Stephen Atkinson of the University of Saskatchewan set about making sure the bears were breathing normally in comfortable positions before beginning their tests. I composed the wild scene out on the tundra with an ultra-wide lens to add a polar dimension of curved, open space. Atkinson was studying the bear's special metabolic adaptations to a state of "walking hibernation" that allows it to go without food for months each summer. Polischuk was measuring levels of toxic organochlorines, such as PCBs and Chlordane, that have doubled in bear's milk and adipose tissue since the sixties. Levels are highest in nursing cubs during the fall, when the mother's weight is low and toxics stored in fat are released into her milk. Of the myriad artificial chemicals introduced into the Arctic, these merit special concern. Their name, *organo*chlorines, defines their purpose to mimic natural compounds and damage central nervous systems in insects. Highly soluble in animal fat, they can biomagnify up the food chain over a million times before reaching polar bears, which are experiencing an unexplained decline in reproductive performance around Hudson Bay. In the South, DDT was detected three decades ago in Adélie penguins. *(Nikon F4, 16mm f2.8 lens, f8 at 1/250 second, Fuji Velvia)*

Biologists weighing polar bear cub, Cape Churchill, Manitoba, Canada; 1993 *p. 107*

After completing several hours of scientific tests, a research team puts a net around the tranquilized cub shown in the previous photographs to weigh it from a sturdy tripod. As I approached the cub with a camera, it raised its head and stared at me. I froze the moment with autofocus and autoexposure. The researchers had taken blood, milk, breath, fat, and hair samples before weighing in the chunky two-year-old at 250 pounds. His mother weighed less than 400 pounds, but would more than double her weight during her next pregnancy. One very scrawny female with two cubs weighed just 213 pounds in late fall, only to be back up to 992 pounds eight months later. Stephen Atkinson is concerned that if global warming lengthens ice-free summers when bears can't hunt seals around Hudson Bay, their seasonal body fat levels may drop below the survival threshold. Resource managers are concerned because nutritionally challenged bears are most likely to seek human food sources. *(Nikon N90, 35–70mm f2.8 lens, SB-25 flash, f5.6 at 1/125 second, Fuji Velvia)*

Riiser-Larsen emperor penguin colony, Riiser-Larsen Ice Shelf, Weddell Sea, Antarctica; 1993 *p. 108*

Bernard Stonehouse of the Scott Polar Research Institute of Cambridge was on the team that discovered this remote emperor colony in 1986 and counted 5,900 breeding pairs. He was also on the staff of the first tourist voyage into the Weddell Sea on the Russian icebreaker *Kapitan Khlebnikov*. Even with him aboard, the colony at latitude 72° south was hard to locate. He eventually found the birds about 6 miles inland from any point we could reach by ship on a reconnaissance flight with a ship-based helicopter. Early the next morning all staff and passengers were landed near the colony to spend the entire day. By 10 A.M. one zealous amateur photographer had shot all forty-seven of the 36-exposure rolls she had brought for the day. I thought I shot a lot with twenty rolls in ten hours. I never considered conserving film as I worked mainly on concepts I first saw in my mind's eye. This image depicts many aspects of emperor behavior in one frame, from the greeting ritual of the adult pair in the foreground, to their large chick begging for a food exchange, to the tiny chick at the far right that is either abandoned or hatched too late. Even with parental care, it has virtually no chance of survival. The season will be too close to winter before it is ready to fledge. I used a Singh-Ray two-stop, soft-edged graduated neutral-density filter to hold detail in the background ice while opening up the exposure on the foreground birds. *(Nikon F4, 35–70mm f2.8 lens, f16 at 1/15 second, Fuji Velvia)*

Emperor penguin exchanging food, Riiser-Larsen colony, Riiser-Larsen Ice Shelf, Weddell Sea, Antarctica; 1993 *p. 108*
Emperor chicks are fully dependent on their parents for six months before they molt into adult plumage and take to the sea. This hungry chick in its last month before fledg-

ing may eat as much as 8 pounds a day of krill, squid, and fish transferred from its parents' stomachs. Fathers incubate the eggs alone for six to eight weeks in winter. Mothers show up from the sea at hatching time to begin food exchanges. I photographed more than twenty food exchanges to get this one shot that clearly shows both birds' beaks and faces along with a catch light in the chick's eye supplied by fill-flash. *(Nikon F4, 80–200mm f2.8 lens, SB-25 flash, f5.6 at 1/250 second, Fuji Velvia)*

Emperor penguin greeting ritual, Cape Crozier Colony, Ross Island, Antarctica; 1992 *p. 109*
When a pair of emperors stopped to greet each other outside their colony, I used a telephoto with fill-flash set to a -1.7 exposure compensation to single them out with clean blacks and whites. I held the rich blue of the jumbled sea ice by using a manual exposure that would have rendered the birds too dark without fill-flash. Their display went on for several minutes with flutelike calls, bowing together, heads alternately raised toward the sky. *(Nikon N90, 80–200mm f2.8 lens, SB-25 flash, f5.6 at 1/250 second, Fuji Velvia)*

Emperor penguin returning to Cape Crozier Colony, Ross Island, Antarctica; 1992 *p. 109*

This emperor may weigh over 60 pounds as it treks back to its colony bloated with food for its chick. I worked hard to catch a bird resolutely goose-stepping with its foot raised. Its steady, rolling gait across the snow reminded me of a tired skier walking across a parking lot in plastic boots after a hard day. Indeed, it probably did have quite a hard ocean journey. Soon after I took this photograph with Dr. Gerald Kooyman, he set up a research camp beside a colony of 20,000 emperors at Cape Washington that I briefly visited. Studies of underwater emperor behavior that he began several years ago, both by scuba-diving observation and remote telemetry, reversed the prevailing assumption that emperors feed close to their colonies. Many travel hundreds of miles on a single food mission. One champion ocean swimmer traveled nearly 900 miles on a month-long foraging journey. *(Nikon N90, 80–200mm f2.8 lens, SB-25 flash, f5.6 at 1/250 second, Fuji Velvia)*

Musk ox on Wrangel Island, Siberian Arctic; 1993 *p. 110*
Musk oxen are singular polar relics of the Pleistocene extinctions. No other land animal so large, so Arctic, and so ancient came through the ice ages so unchanged. While mammoths became extinct, polar bears took to the sea, and caribou ranged south to the temperate latitudes, musk oxen endured a million years of chaotic climate shifts on the tundra of the Far North, protected by their sheer bulk and circle-the-wagons defense against every predator except one. Increasingly sophisticated hunting by native people hastened their disappearance from both Siberia and Alaska before the twentieth century.

Russian scientists believe that musk oxen may have once roamed this uninhabited Arctic island and either died out or migrated to the mainland across the pack ice

during a climatic minimum. After twenty animals were transplanted from Alaska in 1975, all but two died. Although numbers are now up to 250, scientists are concerned about the lack of genetic diversity from just two progeny. Dental irregularities are extremely common. All the present Alaskan musk oxen are descendants of just thirty animals brought from Greenland in 1930.

As I set up a telephoto on the glacier-scoured highlands of the island, this animal stood like a parked truck. When I dropped low to the ground in the same spot to frame it against distant snow peaks, it made a short bluff charge a moment after I captured its direct gaze. *(Nikon F4, 300mm f2.8 lens, f8 at 1/125 second, Fuji Velvia)*

Dwarf mammoth teeth, 3,600 years old, Wrangel Island, Siberian Arctic; 1993 *p. 110*
Zoologist Sergey Vartanyan, whose specialty is snow geese, holds a pair of unfossilized mammoth teeth he recently found in the tundra of Wrangel Island. When carbon-14 dates showed them to be only 3,600 years old, the revolutionary find was the subject of a 1993 article with pictures of these same teeth in *Nature*, the prestigious journal of the biological sciences. The almost mythical creature wandered the tundra when the pharaohs ruled Egypt. In college in the sixties, I was taught that mammoths rapidly became extinct between 18,000 and 11,000 years ago as the Pleistocene ice ages ended and the warm Holocene period, in which we were living, began. I say *were* living, because I no longer believe in the Holocene. We appear to be living in a warmer interglacial period of the Pleistocene epoch that is very much a present reality in the polar regions. *(Nikon F4, 24mm f2.8 lens, SB-25 flash, f8 at 1/8 second, Fuji Velvia)*

Stormy sunset over Wrangel Island, Siberian Arctic; 1993 *p. 111*

In 1976, the year after musk oxen were transplanted, all of Wrangel Island was designated as a nature reserve to protect major breeding areas for polar bears, snow geese, and walrus, as well as many other animals and birds. Visitation is restricted by the Russian science base at Ushakovskoye, founded in 1926. Requests from Arctic tourist ships to come ashore are regularly denied, as they were on the previous traverse of the Northeast Passage by our Russian ship, the *Yamal*. During one rare permitted visit, the base doctor said he was short of certain medical supplies. As staff lecturers, Barbara and I joined a helicopter flight to deliver boxes of the medical supplies they needed, as if they had formally requested them. Thus we were able to negotiate permission for our group of thirty passengers to visit the wild heart of the island.

Another of the *Yamal*'s lecturers was Mikhail Grosswald, chief of earth sciences for the Russian Academy of Sciences. He told me a disturbing story of finding a mammoth tusk eroding out of a stream gully on an earlier tourist visit and deciding to leave it in place. It was missing at the end of the day. Members of the ship's Russian crew had dug it out to saw into sections and sell to passengers. The day after our visit, all passengers were invited to a "colourful Crew Bazaar." Among the items for sale were thin sections of that mammoth tusk for $80 each, plus whole Wrangel walrus tusks for $100.

I made this photograph from the moving ship as we were leaving the island, using a Singh-Ray two-stop graduated neutral-density filter to hold detail in the clouds and the ocean at the same time. *(Nikon F4, 35mm f1.4 lens, f1.4 at 1/250 second, Fuji Velvia push processed to ISO 100)*

Schoolyard in Ushakovskoye village, Wrangel Island, Siberian Arctic; 1993 *p. 111*

The small settlement surrounding the science base of Ushakovskoye is a mixture of transplanted Chukchi Siberian natives and highly educated scientists. The woman walking with her child beyond the schoolyard fence is a doctor who speaks fluent English. Her home is filled with lovely books and posters that depict natural beauty, yet the world outside her window is a depressing morass of mud and abandoned junk so typical of the Russian Arctic. Russian culture since the Bolshevik Revolution has been surprisingly oblivious to the urban blight that appalls almost every visitor. Communism diverted national symbolism away from personally pleasing aesthetics, conditioning Russians to see progress, pride, and utility in scenes that we see as simply ugly. Now that the Soviet Union has collapsed, Russia has the chance to renew the appreciation of pleasing environments it once shared with its Scandinavian neighbors. I tried to seek out the tidiest scene in the village for this image, using a Singh-Ray two-stop graduated neutral-density filter to hold detail in the sky and the foreground. *(Nikon F4, 35mm f1.4 lens, f5.6 at 1/30 second, Fuji Velvia)*

Chukchi children, Wrangel Island, Siberian Arctic; 1993 (photograph by Barbara Cushman Rowell) *p. 111*

When our Russian KA-32 helicopter first landed on Wrangel Island to negotiate permission for our group to visit, we had to wait outside the scientific station to see the person in charge. Meanwhile, Barbara made friends with several Chukchi children whose families had been transplanted to the island from the Siberian mainland after the village of Ushakovskoye was established in 1926. When they posed for her out on the tundra beside the helicopter, she first took a few broad shots that included the whole scene, and then made this tight character study of their faces from a comfortable working distance with a telephoto lens on a tripod. *(Nikon F4, 80–200mm f2.8 lens, f8 at 1/60 second, Fuji Velvia)*

King penguins on the Salisbury Plain, Bay of Isles, South Georgia Island, Subantarctic; 1993 *p. 112*

This idyllic scene of king penguins on a wild grassy plain beneath the icy peaks of South Georgia belies the exploitation of the nineteenth and early twentieth centuries, when sealers who had exhausted the 2 million fur seals on the island within a couple of decades took to marching king penguins by the tens of thousands into vats of boiling oil. Over half a million breeding pairs thrive on the island today, but as recently as 1946 their numbers were estimated at only 12,000. A 600 percent increase to 57,000 in 1979 was due both to the cessation of rendering penguins for oil and to a great upsurge in the ocean food supply owing to the decimation of most of the whales.

I used a wide-angle lens with a Singh-Ray two-stop graduated neutral-density filter to take in a broad scene that would hold a full tonal range in peaks, penguins, grass, and cloud. *(Nikon F4, 24mm f2.8 lens, f8 at 1/125 second, Fuji Velvia)*

King penguins asleep on the Salisbury Plain, Bay of Isles, South Georgia Island, Subantarctic; 1993 *p. 112*

I used a telephoto lens to single out this pair of king penguins and make them appear headless as they slept while incubating eggs on their toes. Chicks hatch about seven weeks after eggs are laid, but remain dependent upon their parents for nearly a year before molting and heading into the sea. Although adult kings may be over 3 feet tall—nearly the height of an emperor penguin—their maximum weight is just about half the emperor's 60 pounds. *(Nikon F4, 80–200mm f2.8 lens, f5.6 at 1/250 second, Fuji Velvia)*

Grytviken whaling station, South Georgia Island, Subantarctic; 1993 *p. 113*

I took this view of the abandoned whaling station of Grytviken from aboard ship as we approached the mountainous coast. With a polarizing filter to help separate distant tonal values and my camera braced on the deck rail, I waited for the frame to fill as we neared the Antarctic's first permanent whaling station. It was founded in 1904, a decade after whalers from Argentina, Britain, and Norway had begun to ply the Southern Ocean. In 1902, a Norwegian whaler named Carl Larsen survived an epic winter with his crew by eating 1,100 Adélie penguins on Paulet Island after his ship was

167

crushed by ice near the Antarctic Peninsula. When he was honored at a banquet in Buenos Aires, he mentioned seeing thousands of whales. Investors then formed an Argentine company, with a license from the British, for Larsen to operate a whaling station on South Georgia with a crew of Norwegians. The plant could process twenty-five giant fin whales up to 60 feet long in twenty-four hours, keeping 300 men busy. It was abandoned in 1965 after processing hundreds of thousands of whales and nearly depleting the Southern Ocean. *(Nikon F4, 85mm f2 lens, f2 at 1/500 second, Fuji Velvia)*

Antarctic fur seal, Salisbury Plain, Bay of Isles, South Georgia Island, Subantarctic; 1993 *p. 113*

I used a telephoto lens to single out this "walking seal" that can move faster on land than a man with a bag of Nikons. Fur seals use all four limbs to move far more quickly than true seals, which hump along with their flippers. The thick, windproof fur that allows these seals to survive in cold lands and seas almost led to their extinction on South Georgia soon after sealers found them. In the first season in 1800, 112,000 fur seals were taken by seventeen ships. By 1822, James Weddell estimated that 1.2 million fur seals had been taken from the island, virtually wiping out the population. The search for more seals to render into oil and fur led to almost simultaneous discoveries of the Antarctic continent by three men in 1820—a Russian, an Englishman, and an American. Soon after the turn of the century, Antarctic fur seals were thought to be extinct after more than 2 million had been killed on South Georgia. In 1933, a few hundred were found living on an offshore island. With the end of hunting and an extra bounty of food from the decimation of the whales, the seals' numbers on South Georgia have now rebounded to over 2 million, such that they constitute the great majority of the world's population. *(Nikon F4, 80–200mm f2.8 lens, f5.6 at 1/250 second, Fuji Velvia)*

Polar bear encounter with sled dog, Cape Churchill, Manitoba, Canada; 1993 *p. 114*

As we watched a polar bear head straight for a sled dog, Dr. James Halfpenny exclaimed, "It's going to happen right in front of us!" The bear looked calm, almost serene, as the dog leapt in the air and jerked against its chain just 50 feet from the open window of the small vehicle from which Barbara and I were taking pictures. The huge male could have dispatched the smaller animal with a casual swat, but didn't. The bear had only come to play with the dog, not to harm it or steal its food. After about twenty minutes, the play ended when the huge, well-insulated bear became overheated and tired.

"There's a lot of misinformation around about these encounters," Halfpenny said. "A local told me that seven of Brian's dogs have been killed by bears this year, but his records show only four in fifteen years. I examined one last year that wasn't eaten and had no marks on it other than a broken neck. It just played too hard with its 1,000-pound friend." *(Nikon F4, 300mm f2.8 lens, f2.8 at 1/250 second, Fuji Velvia push processed to ISO 100)*

Polar bear approaching sled dog, Cape Churchill, Manitoba, Canada; 1993 *p. 115*

Through my telephoto lens I saw a very different scene from the life-and-death encounter that had seemed inevitable as a bear that had been fasting for months approached a tethered dog. For the next eight

rolls, the rare scenario unfolded exactly as our biologist friend Jim Halfpenny had described it the previous evening over dinner. The most experienced Canadian polar bear scientist, Dr. Ian Stirling, had never seen it. Jim, a winter ecologist, had told us with a twinkle in his eye: "You can tell when the bears are out with Brian Ladoon's dogs by the locals' trucks all around with big lenses sticking out the windows. It's about the only place where they can predictably see bears these days without having to pay hundreds of bucks to ride a Tundra Buggy into the controlled area. All the bears that come into town or visit the dump get darted by wardens and put in the polar bear jail. In November when the ice forms on Hudson Bay, they're turned loose and they naturally head out to hunt for seals. The system works pretty well. It's saved a lot of bears from being killed or relocated." *(Nikon F4, 300mm f2.8 lens, f2.8 at 1/250 second, Fuji Velvia push processed to ISO 100)*

Polar bear playing with sled dog, Cape Churchill, Manitoba, Canada; 1993 *p. 115*

We watched in total fascination as the great bear rubbed noses with the dog, tugged on it gently, and rolled it over on the snow. The dog nipped back playfully. Both animals clearly made conscious efforts not to harm each other. I wanted my photos to capture that positive reaching out of one species to another, rather than serve as an image that could be twisted into an icon of savage nature by an editor's clever turn of phrase. I didn't anticipate that the bear's day would end on a very different note. I succeeded so well at showing the bear-dog encounter in single photographs that I felt I had to turn down a *Life* magazine offer to buy just one of these images because I did not want it in print without the rest of the story. *(Nikon F4, 500mm f4 lens, f4 at 1/250 second, Fuji Velvia push processed to ISO 100)*

Polar bear darted by game warden, Cape Churchill, Manitoba, Canada; 1993 *p. 115*

In the evening we returned to see trucks from the Royal Canadian Mounted Police and Manitoba Natural Resources parked near our favorite bear. A shot rang out, the bear ran off, and we followed the officers to the animal spread out in the snow. He was disarmed by the tranquilizer, but conscious enough to lift his great head with eyes that followed us as officers winched him into the bed of a pickup truck filled with debris. He was on his way to the polar bear jail, the officer said, because they had been instructed to take bears attracted by artificial food sources, such as the dog's food, the dogs themselves, or meat dropped to distract the bears during feeding time.

The idea behind the polar bear jail, a holding facility for sixteen bears in solitary confinement plus four family groups, is to provide a neutral or negative experience about approaching human food sources such as the town or its dump. That evening, however, the officers went beyond their mandate to manage bears around populated areas for public safety. Miles from town, they darted all three bears near the dogs. The action began after a bear crawled up onto the filthy bed of a warden's truck that smelled of seal bait used for mechanical bear traps. That bear was put to death; the other two (including this one) were held in the jail.

The issue has become highly controversial. Public safety could of course be wholly maximized by getting rid of all the bears. What's at stake here, though, goes beyond the powerful, unstructured feeling of viewing bears in their natural surroundings to encompass the very nature of the gentle interaction between species that often occurs between bears and dogs, and, more important, between bears and humans. Even though polar bears have the reputation of pursuing humans to the death, Churchill anecdotes of bears avoiding human conflict far outnumber tales of grim encounters. *(Nikon F4, 16mm f2.8 lens, SB-25 flash, f5.6 at 1/15 second, Fuji Velvia)*

Juncture of volcanics and sediments, Royal Society Range, Transantarctic Mountains, Antarctica; 1992 *p. 116*

I stepped back to photograph two geologists walking through this scene of striking diagonal contrasts at the end of a field day beneath a spur of 12,520-foot Mount Rucker in the Royal Society Range. Dr. Terry Wilson of Ohio State University is descending an ice-free valley with her research assistant, Peter Braddock, after plotting the slip directions of hundreds of tiny micro-faults in the light-colored ancient sediments. They hope to gain a better idea about the structural origin of these mountains that may put together another piece of the puzzle about the breakup of the supercontinent Gondwanaland, which began 140 million years ago. Antarctica drifted apart from other pieces that became Africa, Australia, India, and South America.

What do geologists have to do with Antarctic biology? Plenty. After Shackleton's 1908 South Pole expedition brought back coal samples from the Beardmore Glacier, a burning question arose: How did rocks born of swampy vegetation that matches the fossil record of Africa, Australia, India, and South America come to exist on this presently ice-covered continent? *(Nikon N90 35–70mm f2.8 lens, f8 at 1/125 second, Fuji Velvia)*

Weddell seal wired for science, McMurdo Sound, Antarctica; 1992 *p. 117*

Three aspects of Weddell seals make them ideal subjects for scientific study: They have remarkable oxygen-transport systems. They are placid and unafraid of humans. And they are easily "dedicated" to dive and return to holes drilled in the ice miles from their natural ones, enabling them to be precisely studied in the wild.

The tactic of drilling a new ice hole far enough away from existing holes so that a seal can't swim the distance in a single dive was first used by Dr. Gerald Kooyman of the Scripps Institution, who spent years studying Weddells before beginning his work with emperor penguins (see pages 92–93). Kooyman called Weddells the "consummate divers." Dives of up to 93 minutes and depths of nearly 2,000 feet have been recorded—second among mammals only to those of harder-to-study sperm whales and elephant seals.

Dr. Warren Zapol, an anesthesiologist at Massachusetts General Hospital who specializes in respiratory problems, has spent years studying the extraordinary control of blood oxygen levels that Weddells maintain during the most stressful dives. He and the team of researchers he brought to McMurdo Sound surgically wired up the Weddell in this photograph with microcatheters to take blood samples in real-time during dives, laser photospectrometers to monitor oxygen levels in blood and muscle, and more conventional devices to record velocity, depth, pulse, respiration, and EKG readings. I wired a flash unit remotely on the side of the hole to work as a ring light when the seal surfaced to breath, quite unconcerned about my presence. After a few weeks, the researchers removed their devices and released the seal to its old hole. *(Nikon F4, 24mm f2.8 lens, SB-25 flash, f4 at 1/15 second, Fuji Velvia push processed to ISO 100)*

Culturing algae in a cold lab, Crary Laboratory, McMurdo Station, Antarctica; 1992 *p. 117*

Modern scientists working in cold labs are able to test the environmental thresholds of temperature, moisture, and sunlight that permit these plants to grow in an extreme habitat that is strikingly similar, they believe, to that of early Mars. The green stain below the surface on the right edge of this apparently lifeless piece of Beacon sandstone is algae that have been cultured in a laboratory flask by Dr. Sean Turner.

Geology and botany merge in the study of the "cryptogamic" flora of Antarctica—algae and mosses growing in the rocks and ice. Eighteen species were collected by young Joseph Dalton Hooker on his 1839–43 journey aboard the *Erebus* with Sir James Clark Ross (see page 145). Hooker strongly influenced Charles Darwin's developing theory of evolution with his findings, such as the similarity of these tiny plants to ones he later collected in Australia, South Africa, and South America. He incorrectly attributed the floral connection to "the destruction of considerable areas of land" instead of to continental drift, a theory that only gained general acceptance in the 1960s. *(Nikon F4, 60mm f2.8 lens, f22 at 2 seconds, Fuji Velvia)*

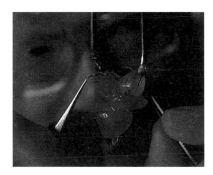

Testing a beating fish heart, Crary Laboratory, McMurdo Station, Antarctica; 1992 *p. 117*

The water of the Ross Sea stays consistently below freezing owing to its salt content. The common Antarctic cod are so cold-adapted that their body temperature is 28.6°F and they die in water above 42°F. Their hearts, however, continue to beat at temperatures a few degrees higher. In this photograph, Ting Wang is studying the beating heart of an Antarctic cod in a controlled laboratory situation as it is being warmed until it stops. I used a macro lens with a combination of natural light through a window with light from a remote flash bounced from two

reflectors. Wang's work is part of an ongoing study, led by cryobiologist Dr. Arthur DeVries for the past thirty years, of the functioning of natural "antifreeze" proteins in Antarctic fish (see pages 96–97). In the same lab another researcher was using a chromatograph to try to identify the chemical compounds essential to the antifreeze. Possible practical applications include tomatoes and salmon for cold climates spliced with antifreeze genes and ice cream that won't have those crunchy crystals when it is refrozen. *(Nikon N90, 60mm f2.8 lens, SB-25 flash, f5.6 at 1/30 second, Fuji Velvia)*

Dr. Robert Wharton beside algae in frozen Lake Hoare, Dry Valleys, Transantarctic Mountains, Antarctica; 1992 *p. 117*

The small clump of algae trapped in the ice beside Dr. Robert Wharton of the Desert Research Institute of Reno, Nevada, has quite a life history. The Dry Valleys appear to be the most lifeless places on earth, so much like the surface of a foreign planet that he has merged his studies with the NASA Mars program (see pages 83, 124–25). The realization that liquid water is an absolutely nonnegotiable requirement for life as we know it led him to spend many seasons exploring Lake Hoare, a 2.5-mile-long freshwater lake. Beneath a permanent cover of at least 10 feet of ice, waters well above freezing support a surprisingly thick benthic mat of algal growth shielded from the harsh Antarctic environment. This piece of live algae drifted upward to become trapped on top of the winter surface ice during the few summer weeks when some surface melting occurs. *(Nikon N90, 24mm f2.8 lens, f16 at 1/60 second, Fuji Velvia)*

Todd Skinner free climbing on Proboscis, Cirque of the Unclimbables, Northwest Territories, Canada; 1992 *p. 118*
Todd Skinner leads up the sheer 2,000-foot face of Proboscis using just his fingers and toes for upward progress. He avoids the little hanging ecosystem to his right, because he has previously checked it out and knows it is too fragile to support his weight. Far more species of plants grow on this single cliff than on the entire Antarctic continent.

Todd is tied to a rope belayed for safety from below by Paul Piana, while I am hanging from a separate rope. We placed it days earlier with frequent use of direct aids (standing in stirrups hooked to anchors in the rock) so that Todd and Paul could use it to rehearse the hardest gymnastic moves before trying to free-climb the entire face with ropes for safety only. I used the fixed rope to photograph the leader from dramatic angles at critical moments as Todd and Paul alternated leads up the longest stretch of extreme free climbing ever done at the time (800 feet of pitches rated 5.12 and 5.13). While tied to mechanical ascenders, I hung onto the rope with one hand, leaned out, and shot pictures in autofocus mode with the other hand. On the easier upper half of the climb where there were no fixed ropes, we alternated leads as a threesome. *(Nikon 8008s, 24mm f2.8 lens, f5.6 at 1/60 second, Fuji Velvia)*

Moss campion, Cirque of the Unclimbables, Northwest Territories, Canada; 1992 *p. 118*

Whenever I see one of these little cushion plants in bloom, my heart skips a beat and my mind wanders to other wild places where I have seen it. Circumpolar in distribution, moss campion often clings to sheer rock faces well above other flowering plants. It extends south of the true Arctic Circle into life zones above timberline in the Alps, the Rockies, and other northern temperate ranges. Here, it grows atop "reindeer moss," a popular misnomer for a common circumpolar lichen that grows in thick mats.

Any color appears more saturated beside a darker tone, and I maximized the intensity of this bloom on a block of granite below Proboscis by framing it against a jagged, diagonal shadow that I knew would go black on my film. I was using Fuji Velvia, which is designed to drop shadows quickly to black but still hold good detail in a tonal range equal to that of other top slide films. The name Velvia is a contraction of "velvet media." *(Nikon F4, 55mm f2.8 lens, f32 at 4 seconds, Fuji Velvia)*

The Southeast Face of Proboscis, Cirque of the Unclimbables, Northwest Territories, Canada; 1992 *p. 118*
As Paul Piana, Todd Skinner, and I drove to the Far North to attempt a new climb on this spectacular rock wall, days became longer, sun angles lower, and vegetation less complex. Species dropped away with each passing mile. Our gradual entry into a simplified subarctic landscape sped up considerably as we flew the final miles from the Yukon to a campsite below the peak in a valley that looked like a huge Japanese garden. Although still south of the Arctic Circle, we were camped at 6,000 feet, high above timberline, in a clearly Arctic life zone.

One morning, I hiked down to this unnamed lake before dawn. I searched the banks for a composition that would combine a fine reflection with the sense of ordered simplicity the whole area gave me. As the sun rose, my first compositions were somewhat rushed and cluttered. I had placed the small iceberg on the left against the bright reflection instead of within the shadow, and I had not yet framed the foreground rock into a strong diagonal coming out of the corner of the image. *(Nikon 8008s, 20mm f4 lens, f16 at 1/8 second, Fuji Velvia)*

Moonrise from the Cirque of the Unclimbables, Northwest Territories, Canada; 1992 *p. 119*
Moments after sunset, I saw the moon rise over a distant ridge from the face of Proboscis, where we had been working with fixed ropes to prepare our route for the final ascent. I didn't have a long lens with me, but I knew how to get a second chance at the moon coming over the crest. I reset the moon by descending the ropes and running down to get my lens in camp. Minutes later, I caught the second moonrise with a 300mm lens plus teleconverter for an effective 600mm. To make the sharpest image in dim light, I devised a rock-solid support by propping both the camera and the end of the lens in cradles of rocks atop a boulder. With such extreme magnification, I stopped down to f22 for full depth of field and set the exposure by a spot meter reading off the moon itself, which is as bright as daylight when high in the sky, but dimmer when on the horizon. *(Nikon F4, 300mm f2.8 lens, 2X teleconverter, f22 at 1 second, Fuji Velvia)*

Paul Piana bivouacking on Proboscis, Cirque of the Unclimbables, Northwest Territories, Canada; 1992 *p. 119*

We reached the top of the 2,000-foot face of Proboscis in light snow flurries in the dark, where we bivouacked on a ridge crest no wider than a chair. The knife-edge dropped 2,000 feet on both sides. With the wind roaring and the temperature in the teens, we tied ourselves in and lay down as best we could, heads hung over one valley and feet draped over the other. Before dawn, I quietly got out my camera and set it up with fill-flash on a tiny Gitzo tripod. Paul couldn't believe his ears when he heard my shutter. When he looked to see what was happening, I caught his eye peering out of his bivouac sack and asked him to hold the pose as the sun rose into a thankfully clearing sky. *(Nikon 8008s, 20mm f4 lens, SB-25 flash, f5.6 at 1/15 second, Fuji Velvia)*

Midnight sun over the Weddell Sea, Antarctica; 1993 *p. 120*
After ten days of cloudy skies aboard the Russian icebreaker *Kapitan Khlebnikov*, the evening sun appeared over the pack ice of the Weddell Sea for a few hours. As the rapidly moving ship crunched through the ice, I used several tricks to shoot sharp images off the bow. A wide-angle lens diminished the effective motion, and an f1.4 aperture gave me a 1/1000 shutter speed on fine-grained Velvia pushed to gain extra film speed. A three-stop graduated neutral-density filter was used to hold back the bright sky. We were detouring from a direct route to an emperor colony to break out the RRS *Bransfield*, a British Antarctic Survey research and supply ship bound for Halley Station that was stuck in the ice at latitude 71° 36' south. It was not a true rescue, because the spring pack ice was melting and the ship would have soon freed itself. Such was not the case for Shackleton, whose *Endurance* was crushed in the pack ice of the Weddell Sea in 1915, setting the stage for an epic self-rescue. He and his twenty-eight men drifted for months on ice floes and in an open lifeboat before boldly crossing the wild seas to South Georgia Island. Despite later explorations by icebreaker

and aircraft, the Weddell Sea remains the least-explored major body of water on earth. *(Nikon F4, 35mm f1.4 lens, f1.4 at 1/1000 second, Fuji Velvia push processed to ISO 100)*

Shackleton's grave at Grytviken, South Georgia Island, Subantarctic; 1993 *p. 120*
I used an ultra-wide 16mm lens to capture polar scientist Dr. Bernard Stonehouse leading a toast to Sir Ernest Shackleton at his grave beside the whaling station of Grytviken. He died at the age of 47 in 1922 of a massive heart attack, the night after reaching Grytviken for the first time since his epic journey to South Georgia in an open boat six years earlier. He was aboard his new ship, *Quest*, at the start of yet another Antarctic expedition. The crew put his body on a ship to go back to England, but when his widow learned what had happened, she had his body taken off in Montevideo and returned to South Georgia, where she felt he rightfully belonged. Seeing his grave in a little cemetery among men of the southern seas reminded me of the legendary newspaper advertisement that he may or may not have written to find men for his 1914 Weddell Sea journey: "Men wanted for Hazardous Journey. Small wages, bitter cold, long months of complete darkness, constant danger, safe return doubtful. Honour and recognition in case of success." *(Nikon F4, 16mm f2.8 lens, f5.6 at 1/60 second, Fuji Velvia)*

Launching a Zodiac raft, Thule Island, South Sandwich Islands, Subantarctic; 1993 *p. 121*

The day we reached Thule Island began with tea and pastry in the lounge of our 18,000-ton icebreaker, *Kapitan Khlebnikov*. An aerobics group met in the gym and a biologist gave a slide show on penguins in the lecture theater, where *A River Runs Through It* would be shown in the evening. When we reached Thule in the afternoon, six Zodiac rafts were launched to take passengers ashore. Only during these brief minutes in open boats did our journey from the Weddell Sea to South Georgia bear even the faintest resemblance to Shackleton's epic trip. I caught a group of staff and passengers launching a raft in the late evening by using fill-flash with a manual exposure for the bright highlights on the water. *(Nikon F4, 35–70mm f2.8 lens, SB-25 flash, f4 at 1/125 second, Fuji Velvia)*

Emperor penguin and icebreaker, Akta Bay, Weddell Sea, Antarctica; 1993 (photograph by Barbara Cushman Rowell) *p. 121*
While returning to the icebreaker *Kapitan Khlebnikov* from an emperor penguin colony in a blizzard, my wife, Barbara Cushman Rowell, stopped to photograph a single emperor penguin standing hundreds of yards away from its colony on a trail to the ice edge. She set up a telephoto lens on a tripod and waited until the penguin turned its head in the right way to provide a strong black-and-white counterpoint to the only other object in the simple scene. For more information on the scenario, see photographs on pages 17, 41, and 85. *(Nikon F4, 80–200mm f2.8 lens, f5.6 at 1/30 second, Fuji Velvia)*

Midnight sun on tabular iceberg, Weddell Sea, Antarctica; 1993 *p. 121*

Every visitor to the Weddell Sea is captivated by the sight of huge tabular icebergs that break off from vast ice shelves along the coast and float around for years. This berg was estimated to be 2 miles long and 800 feet thick, but some exceed 100 miles. To photographers, these blocks of freshwater land ice in the sea provide visions of temporal beauty to be singled out in fine light. To businessmen or politicians, they may be considered a resource to be exploited. In 1977, a Saudi prince formed a company to tow Antarctic bergs to the Middle East—an idea doomed by distance. Future ice transport to arid parts of Australia or South America, however, is contemplated.

To thirty-two Russian and American scientists who spent four months drifting 400 miles on Ice Station Weddell in 1992, ice became a platform for study of the Weddell Sea's role in the global circulation of more than half of the world's cold-bottom waters that greatly affect climate. The northerly flow of these supercooled waters is over a hundred times greater than the combined flow of all the world's rivers into the oceans. The scientists chose a block of sea ice less than 10 feet thick and 2 miles square from which to closely monitor the sea, but they had helicopters ready to lift them atop the nearest tabular iceberg in case their floe began to break up. I shot this photograph with a fast telephoto during brief seconds when the sun shone only on the berg. *(Nikon F4, 85mm f2 lens, f2 at 1/500 second, Fuji Velvia push processed to ISO 100)*

Sirius Sled Patrol crossing frozen Youngsund Fjord at 74° north, Northeast Greenland National Park; 1993 *p. 122*
A Danish soldier runs beside his heavily loaded dogsled as the sun sets over a frozen fjord. I asked him to try to keep his shadow blocking my camera to create a photograph with vivid backlighting and no lens flare. I was lying down on the runners with my face inches from the ice using an ultra-wide 15mm rectilinear lens. He and his partner

patrol sections of a national park a hundred times larger than Yellowstone. The region is uninhabited except for about forty men in a few weather stations and the Sirius Sled Patrol, which maintains surveillance over 8,000 miles of coastline that comes within 400 miles of the North Pole. In 1931, five Norwegian fur trappers persuaded their government to claim northern Greenland. Two years later, the World Court at The Hague confirmed Danish sovereignty only so long as Denmark showed "the will to possess" by maintaining official presence well beyond the few Danish government personnel in Scoresbysund, less than halfway up the coast. The Danes thus created a ground patrol, which foiled Nazi landings on the coast during World War II and later became known as the Sirius Sled Patrol. Since the huge park was created in 1973, the patrol has also monitored wildlife and the tiny amount of tourism. *(Nikon N90, 15mm f3.5 lens, f5.6 at 1/500 second, Fuji Velvia)*

Lars Ulsoe of the Sirius Sled Patrol with his lead dog, Northeast Greenland National Park; 1993 *p. 123*
To capture Lars Ulsoe hugging his lead dog before harnessing his team at dawn I used fill-flash to light the shadows while exposing for the pink glow on the sunlit peaks. Ulsoe, who was once an exchange student in Minnesota, seeks out exotic challenges that will further his personal growth. He comes from a part of the world that has always lacked the resources to keep its brightest young men at home. Ulsoe was named the patrol's leader the season after I made this photograph.

Sled patrol members are handpicked from thousands of military volunteers who claim to be willing to endure hardship in exchange for the wild experience. Those who pass rigid medical and psychological testing must accept twenty-five months of duty with round-the-clock responsibilities and no leave or days off. They raise their own dogs and make their own harnesses and sleds—"whereby it is ensured that they will be capable of repairing these items during the long journey," in the words of their commander, who touts the superiority of dogs to aircraft or tracked vehicles because "the dog requires no repair shops or stocks of spare parts and, should lack of fuel or spare part problems arise, it will be able to participate in the acquisition of these items." *(Nikon N90, 80–200mm f2.8 lens, SB-25 flash, f5.6 at 1/30 second, Fuji Velvia)*

Northern lights over Sirius Sled Patrol camp at 74° north, Northeast Greenland National Park; 1993 *p. 123*

Soon after Lars Ulsoe and Tommy Pederson set up a special tent anchored to the back of their dogsled, the northern lights began to dance in curtains all around us. I set up a tripod with an electronic remote release on my camera that enabled me to set off timed long exposures and return to the tent. Photographing the aurora always involves a trade-off. Fast films above ISO 400 do a better job freezing the motion of the dancing banners, but give the sky and landscape a harsh and grainy look. Slow films tend to lose the fine shapes of the best displays, while holding far better detail and tonal range. Kodak Lumiere 100 pushed one stop gives me the best compromise. It also holds the sky true blue during long exposures, unlike Fuji Velvia, which shifts toward green because of reciprocity failure. Here I made the further compromise of losing considerable shutter speed to gain enough depth of field to hold both tent and stars in focus. *(Nikon F4, 35mm f1.4 lens, f5.6 at 6 minutes, Kodak Lumiere 100 push processed to ISO 200)*

Arctic hares at night, Daneborg, Northeast Greenland National Park; 1993 *p. 123*

These very large hares remain white and active throughout the year on the northeast coast of Greenland. They often weigh more than the arctic fox that prey on their young. I found them impossible to approach closely enough to photograph during the day, but virtually unafraid at night, when they gathered in large groups near the dogs tethered beside the Sirius headquarters at Daneborg. I was able to make sharp night photographs of them thanks to an infrared sensor that operates through my flash unit to provide autofocus in the dark. *(Nikon N90, 80–200mm f2.8 lens, SB-25 flash, f11 at 1/60 second, Kodak Lumiere 100 push processed to ISO 200)*

Sand dunes of Victoria Valley, Dry Valleys, Transantarctic Mountains, Antarctica; 1992 *p. 124*

Viewed from a distance, the arid, shifting sands of the Dry Valleys appear as if they should be warm to the touch. On this spring morning they were close to their annual mean temperature of -4°F. The sands form near the end of long valleys where high winds laden with grains of rock scraped from the Transantarctic Mountains drop much of their load as they lift over a final ridge toward the Ross Sea. The juxtaposition of glaciers beside sand dunes was hardly new to me. I had seen it many times while exploring the "Third Pole," as the Himalayan region is often called by geographers. The arid Tibetan Plateau that sits in

the rain shadow of the Himalaya has similar valleys where drifting sands abide with ice and snow in a world beyond the reach of all but the hardiest plants and lichens. *(Nikon F4, 20mm f4 lens, f16 at 1/30 second, Fuji Velvia)*

Mummy Pond, Dry Valleys, Transantarctic Mountains, Antarctica; 1992 *p. 124*

One October morning, four of us walked 20 miles along the floor of the Taylor Valley. Soft earth tones of rock dusted with snow were periodically interrupted by dazzling slabs of turquoise ice, set into the rough landscape like polished stones in a giant necklace. One of these frozen lakes was Mummy Pond, named for the naturally freeze-dried mummy seals found near its shores (see page 43). It seemed an unlikely place for the merger of two extremes of scientific research—the probing of the distant past and the priming of future human endeavor. My hiking partner, Dr. Robert Wharton, had given me copies of papers he had written about these lakes as analogs for life on Mars, along with a scrawled note of premature thanks for helping his quest to "push back the frontiers of ignorance and prepare the way for Mars." NASA had lost its budget for a major Mars mission. Lakes like Mummy Pond are believed to resemble the last refuges of life on Mars. Traces of water have been detected at the Martian poles, and evidence of life may exist in habitats like the lakes of the Dry Valleys. Imagine if an unmanned mission from another solar system scooped up some hard rocks without cryptoendolithic life from the ridge above the pond and flew home. Those beings might well conclude that Earth was a dead planet. *(Nikon F4, 20mm f4 lens, f16 at 1/30 second, Fuji Velvia)*

Patterned ground in upper Taylor Valley, Dry Valleys, Transantarctic Mountains, Antarctica; 1992 *p. 125*

On a flight through the Dry Valleys in a Vietnam-style Huey helicopter, I spotted an unusually fine display of "patterned ground" made up of thousands of interlocking polygons on the floor of an arid valley. Veteran navy pilot Beez Bohner cut a slow circle so that I could open the rear door and not have to shoot through the glass. Helicopters vibrate more than fixed-wing aircraft, so I used a very fast lens to maintain a 1/2000 shutter speed. Active patterned ground only occurs in extremely cold places where the average annual temperature is below freezing. Most of the less-defined polygons seen on flat erosion surfaces high in the Rockies and the Sierra are relics of a colder era. Long-term frost wedging and cracking creates unsorted polygons like those of dried mud, which also breaks into regular patterns owing to a difference in surface and base stresses. *(Nikon F4, 35mm f1.4 lens, f1.4 at 1/2000 second, Fuji Velvia push processed to ISO 100)*

Blood Fall, Taylor Valley, Dry Valleys, Transantarctic Mountains, Antarctica; 1992 *p. 125*

Coming upon a huge frozen waterfall in the Dry Valleys seemed as improbable as finding a lake on top of a dune in the Sahara. If the temperature in the deserts of the American Southwest dropped to Antarctic levels, a similar feature would not occur. In the polar latitudes, because the midday sun does not rise more than halfway in the sky, steep ice faces can experience

172

surface melt at air temperatures near 0°F while level ice fields stay frozen. The reddish colors of Blood Fall at the snout of the Taylor Glacier are caused by its brief summer flow contacting mineral salts deposited by an ancient lake. When I arrived in early spring, when there was not a drop of melt, I set my camera on a tripod to sharply freeze the frozen scene. I also used a Singh-Ray two-stop soft-edged graduated neutral-density filter to darken the sky and emphasize the red color in the fall. *(Nikon F4, 35–70mm f2.8 lens, f16 at 1/15 second, Fuji Velvia)*

Galen Rowell climbing rock face in the Asgard Range, Dry Valleys, Transantarctic Mountains, Antarctica; 1992 (photograph by Jules Uberuaga) *p. 125*
While climbing up the ridge of a peak that rises 6,000 feet above the Taylor Valley, I looked over the edge of its sheer south face and saw exposed buttresses deeply eroded by the wind. The hard granitic rock called dolerite was sculpted into horns, plates, and buckets that formed a virtual ladder up the steepest sections. Before climbing out onto the prow to experience vertical rock in such a wild, cold place, I set up my tripod on a small ledge below the ridge and asked my partner, Jules Uberuaga, to click the shutter as I was silhouetted on the horizon. A manual exposure for the bright sky guaranteed that the profile of the shadowed face would go black on film. *(Nikon N90, 24mm f2.8 lens, f11 at 1/60 second, Fuji Velvia)*

Flipper of a mummy seal, Taylor Valley, Dry Valleys, Transantarctic Mountains, Antarctica; 1992 *p. 125*

On my first walks past the mummy seals of the Dry Valleys, all my photographs (see page 43) were conceived as "immature subjects"—my term for a subject that the viewer does not already know well. Such subjects need to be presented clearly and wholly to maximize comprehension of new information, as in children's books or adult stories of new discoveries. After photographing many complete crabeater seals in this unusual setting, I decided to approach them as mature subjects that allow a viewer's mind to fill in perceptual gaps. As my own familiarity increased, I saw a visual metaphor that guided the way I composed this photograph of a particularly eroded seal. Its extended flipper set against cold peaks reminded me of a scene at a destroyed monastery beneath Mount Everest in Tibet where I had come across the severed hand of a statue of Sakyamuni Buddha extended in a similar gesture. Gone was the usual monk's begging bowl that Sakyamuni holds, as it is here. While lying down to isolate this final gesture of a sentient being frozen in time, I thought about how Buddhists interpret Sakyamuni's other hand touching the ground as witness to the earth's emptiness. *(Nikon N90, 55mm f2.8 lens, f22 at 1/8 second, Fuji Velvia)*

Evening clouds over Arakamchechen Island, Chukchi Peninsula, Siberia; 1993 *p. 126*
When I came to Arakamchechen Island to photograph its walrus colony (see page 46), I was struck by the raw beauty of its truly Arctic tundra. The island is, at latitude 65° north, a bit south of the Arctic Circle, but well within the 50°F summer isotherm of Arctic climate that dips far below the circle to include most of the northern Bering Sea. Before communism, the wild island was the province of a single powerful shaman who hung himself when he was deposed. State reindeer farming was introduced and continues today on some parts of the island. Near the walrus colony, I kept an eye

on the green glow of the tundra in the afternoon sun, knowing that what I saw was not what I would get on film—yet. The direct sun that backlit the translucent grass would cause flares in my lens, while the ominous dark sky was actually brighter than the more vivid-appearing tundra. I spot-metered a two-stop exposure difference between grass and sky and used a three-stop Singh-Ray graduated neutral-density filter over my lens to make the sky one stop darker than the tundra. Then I waited for the clouds to barely hide the sun so it wouldn't cause lens flares, but would still be bright enough to backlight the grass. *(Nikon F4, 35–70mm f2.8 lens, f8 at 1/30 second, Fuji Velvia)*

Chukchi woman of Yanrakynnot, Chukchi Peninsula, Siberia; 1993 (photograph by Barbara Cushman Rowell) *p. 126*
Barbara made this portrait at a Chukchi reindeer festival on the open tundra about 2 miles from the depressing village of Yanrakynnot. The previous evening, we had gone on a staff helicopter flight from the *Yamal* to negotiate permission with the village leader. Rundown buildings were set in muddy tundra littered with rusting hulks of vehicles, oil drums, and open containers spewing chemicals into the soil. The festival site, however, was a step into the past— and, I hope, the future—of people who had been forced to live in an ugly commune at the extreme northeastern tip of Siberia after being nomadic reindeer herders since the eleventh century. After the cold war ended, old-fashioned herding began anew. Chukchi tribesmen in traditional reindeer suits herded 2,500 reindeer to the festival site, where a number were slaughtered and cooked over an open fire. Barbara used a telephoto lens to avoid directly intruding into the scene as she singled out this old Chukchi woman whose face was lined with tattoos from the days before communism. Too arthritic to walk without help, the matriarch was quite content to sit outside all

day, watching her people enjoy their old ways. *(Nikon F4, 80–200mm f2.8 lens, f5.6 at 1/60 second, Fuji Velvia)*

Tracked vehicle near Yanrakynnot, Chukchi Peninsula, Siberia; 1993 *p. 127*
While spending a day at a Chukchi reindeer festival, we watched an increasingly tipsy local driver dash back and forth across the tundra from town in an old Soviet armored personnel carrier. In the distance is a government fox farm with thousands of animals fed a quota of wild meat that villagers obtain by hunting whales and walrus. Since the end of the cold war, the Chukchis have been given the right to resume many of their traditional ways, which have been passed down by word of mouth. Few of the present generation, however, were ever taught how to practice those old ways apart from the Soviet influence of radio, TV, snowmobiles, and helicopters to travel to and from remote reindeer camps. With an eroded old sense of the sacred and poor enforcement of modern regulations, both the system and this driver may be headed for a crash. *(Nikon N90, 80–200mm f2.8 lens, f4 at 1/500 second, Fuji Velvia push processed to ISO 100)*

Chukchi reindeer herder, Chukchi Peninsula, Siberia; 1993 *p. 127*
I caught this Chukchi reindeer herder unaware of my camera as he gazed off into a herd of 2,500 reindeer, deciding which animal to cull next. My camera was sitting on a tripod with a telephoto lens focused on

him, while I kept a finger on the shutter and pretended not to be looking his way. The antlers on the ground are from several deer he and two partners had lassoed by the antlers, wrestled to the ground, and butchered for an ongoing village festival just minutes earlier. In the old days, the people of the Chukchi village of Uelen would begin a spring festival with a sacrificial offering of reindeer meat placed on the ice of the still-frozen Bering Sea. As Yuri Rytkheu, a native of Uelen, described it for *National Geographic*, the offerings "eventually would sink through the melting ice and be received by the spirits of the whales, walruses, and other sea creatures that my people hunted." In 1994, Russian scientists revealed controversial evidence that leads them to believe humans inhabited northern Siberia 500,000 years ago. *(Nikon F4, 80–200mm f2.8 lens, f4 at 1/125 second, Fuji Velvia)*

Vehicle tracks near Uelen village, Cape Dezhnev, Chukchi Peninsula, Siberia; 1993 *p. 127*

I made this photograph of tundra ravaged by all-terrain vehicles from a helicopter near the most easterly point of Asia, just outside the village of Uelen. Many Chukchi natives now drive as much as possible for work and fun. Some use motorcycles or three-wheelers, while others have access to old military vehicles. It will take hundreds, possibly thousands, of years for this fresh damage to heal in the short growing season of the Arctic climate. During Stalin's purges, Uelen became a commune into which Chukchi herders themselves were herded against their will, along with a contingent of marine Chukchi moved out of their coastal villages for security reasons to fortify the cape. When *National Geographic* assigned Chukchi writer Yuri Rytkheu, born in Uelen, to write an article published in 1983, he quoted a young woman he met herding reindeer out in the wilds not long after she had returned from school in the city: "The tundra is the very best place to

be. Here one has the real sense of freedom, where there are no restrictions, such as where to cross the street—or the river." For the people of the Russian Arctic, the new freedom has its price. *(Nikon F4, 35mm f1.4 lens, f1.4 at 1/500 second, Fuji Velvia)*

Wreck of the *Bahia Paraiso* floating near Palmer Station, Antarctic Peninsula; 1991 *p. 128*

As the *Professor Molchanov* neared the wreck of the Argentine ship *Bahia Paraiso*, I was on the bridge to hear a voice over the radio demand, "Will the white ship approaching Palmer Station please identify itself. We don't recognize your flag." The Soviet Union had just fallen, and two days earlier the crew of the first Soviet ship chartered for Antarctic tourism had anchored in a bay, pulled out the vodka, lowered the flag, chiseled the hammer and sickle off the stern, and raised a hand-sown Russian flag. Palmer officials acted very concerned as the Russians calmly worked past large icebergs to anchor closer to Palmer than any previous ship of its size. They had a right to be. In 1989, the *Bahia Paraiso* had ripped open its hull as it neared Palmer, spilling over 150,000 gallons of fuel oil that contaminated the bay and beaches frequented by tens of thousands of penguins and seabirds. The ship carried supplies for an Argentine scientific base as well as eighty-one tourists, who were safely rescued. Whether the event qualifies as a major ecological disaster has yet to be determined. The fuel dissipated more quickly than expected, and visible impact on the shores and in the water was gone three years later when I made this photograph with a telephoto from our passing ship. However, 60,000 gallons remained in the hull until removed by a later recovery operation funded by the Netherlands after the Argentines had waffled for years. Ongoing studies are monitoring the distribution and long-term effects of the toxins released in the hydrocarbons. *(Nikon F4, 80–200mm f2.8 lens, f2.8 at 1/500 second, Fuji Velvia push processed to ISO 100)*

Trash dumped in the sea at Argentina's Esperanza science base, Antarctic Peninsula; 1993 *p. 128*

I was shocked to see fresh trash, some of it toxic, dumped into the sea at this Argentine base built into the edge of an Adélie penguin colony. Rocks amidst the penguins are spray-painted with red numbers that minimally aid a scientist to identify clusters of birds, but maximally affect the experience of those hoping to see a pristine Antarctica. Penguins were killed to feed the base's dogs until a decade ago. Each wave of Antarctic visitation has created its own brand of lasting impact, from the sealers, to the whalers, to the explorers, to the scientists, and now to the tourists, who to date have caused far less impact than the earlier groups, partly because they live aboard ships that take everything away. Tourist reports and photographs of ongoing impact have been a major factor in improving the ways that bases are managed. The International Association of Antarctica Tour Operators has established strict guidelines for visitor conduct that were recently accepted under the terms of the Antarctic Treaty. Visitors must not approach animals too closely, walk on fragile vegetation, or take anything with them except their own litter and human waste. *(Nikon F4, 20mm f4 lens, f11 at 1/30 second, Fuji Velvia)*

Iceberg in Paradise Bay, Antarctic Peninsula; 1991 *p. 129*

The raw beauty of this photograph took me by surprise when my film was processed. I'd forgotten it, because I had simply lifted

my camera to my eye and snapped a few frames on automatic with Matrix metering from the bow of the *Professor Molchanov*. As we passed by this small berg under an ominous sky, anyone watching me would have doubted that I visualized it in the conceptual manner that I teach in photo workshops. Consciously, I didn't. Just as a learned dance routine becomes wired into one's motor nerves, so does seeing photographic compositions. The concept can be just as much there in a casual performance, but one that comes only after lots of mindful practice. In fact, I had rehearsed for the simple act of snapping this picture by adjusting a graduated neutral-density filter on a telephoto lens to hold the darkness above the horizon, while opening up a clean exposure for passing ice in the plankton-rich black waters of the Antarctic summer. *(Nikon F4, 85mm f2 lens, f2 at 1/1000 second, Fuji Velvia)*

Hot spring in the crater of Deception Island, Antarctic Peninsula; 1991 *p. 129*

Tourists from a ship anchored in a sheltered bay on Deception Island take an incongruous swim in seawater warmed to about 90°F by geothermal heat. Depending upon the level of volcanic activity, the temperature varies from too cold for swimming to over 110°F. The flooded caldera of the intermittently active volcano can make either the best anchorage in Antarctica or the worst. Ships have fled with their paint blistered during sudden flare-ups, and science bases built by the British, Argentines, and Chileans were destroyed by eruptions during an especially active period between 1967 and 1970. *(Nikon F4, 35–70mm f2.8 lens, SB-25 flash, f5.6 at 1/60 second, Fuji Velvia)*

Gentoo penguin on rusting trash beside Paradise Bay, Antarctic Peninsula; 1991 *p. 129*

The beauty of Paradise Bay, where I also took the iceberg photograph on this page, is marred by an abandoned Chilean base with stacks of leaking drums and other trash. When a gentoo penguin stood atop a rusty drum, I saw it as an icon of the clash between a pristine Antarctic and human intrusions. I quietly waited off to the side with a telephoto lens on a tripod set to hold full sharpness on both the penguin and the drum. I wanted to capture a moment when the bird was looking into the distance attentively.

Chile has built seven scientific bases on the Antarctic Peninsula to undertake limited studies of marine biology and monitor weather, earthquakes, and auroral displays. The United States has only Palmer Station on the peninsula and makes no land claims. Chile, Argentina, and Britain have overlapping claims to the entire peninsula plus a wedge of land going all the way to the South Pole. *(Nikon F4, 80–200mm f2.8 lens, f11 at 1/60 second, Fuji Velvia)*

Circling all the world's time zones at the North Pole, Arctic Ocean; 1993 *p. 130*

Robert Peary's vague and contested account of his 1909 expedition claims he was too exhausted at the pole to realize that he had achieved his life's goal. He goes on to say, "If it were possible for a man to arrive at the North Pole without being utterly exhausted, body and brain, he would doubtless enjoy a series of unique sensations and reflections." After we arrived on August 31,

1993, on the Russian icebreaker *Yamal*, I made this photograph with a very wide-angle lens of the crew and thirty-one passengers dancing arm-in-arm through all the world's time zones. The group soon broke up to drink champagne, have a barbecue, take portraits by a North Pole sign, or seek individual whimsies. I made the preplanned landscape photograph on page 22, donned shorts for a circular run through the time zones, took a very short polar plunge into the open water at the stern, and underwent a more gradual rewarming in the ship's sauna. *(Nikon F4, 16mm f2.8 lens, f8 at 1/125 second, Fuji Velvia)*

GPS (Global Positioning Satellite) read-out forty minutes after arriving at the North Pole, Arctic Ocean; 1993 *p. 130*

The Russian crew of the *Yamal* "found" the North Pole by navigating with a state-of-the-art GPS (Global Positioning Satellite) readout. Robert Peary claimed to have reached the pole in 1909 on latitude readings derived wholly from solar observations. Our crew and staff seriously doubted that Peary could have gotten near the pole by solar observations uncorrected by the longitude information used by every other successful polar explorer. The Russian captain who had been on six of the eleven successful polar journeys by surface ship was emphatic that Peary would have had no clear idea where he was. Peary himself had described the ice drifting silently miles off course. Even his staunchest modern supporter, the Navigation Foundation of Maryland, acknowledges that Peary drifted far to the west on his final journey without knowing it. Their claim of a sudden eastward drift exactly negating the effect is an event an astrophysicist might term a singularity.

I had a rude surprise when I returned to the bridge to photograph our GPS readout at the pole, forty minutes after we had arrived. The readings indicated we had drifted nearly a mile from the pole at a speed of 1.5 knots (1.7 mph), yet the world outside appeared perfectly still. *(Nikon F4, 55mm f2.8 lens, f11 at 1/4 second, Fuji Velvia)*

Nuclear reactor on the Russian icebreaker *Yamal*, en route to the North Pole, Arctic Ocean; 1993 *p. 130*

I took many pictures inside the nuclear reactor room when passengers were given tours during stops, but ended up preferring this ultra-wide image taken by holding my camera steady against an observation window. Before deciding to travel by nuclear vessel, we asked many questions. What level of radiation would we experience? A nuclear physicist on the first tourist voyage had monitored levels that were below what an air traveler receives from background cosmic rays on a polar flight to Europe. Were we supporting nuclear power by participating, or, worse yet, upping the odds of a future Chernobyl? The answers were uncertain, but one convincing argument was that in the present upheaval after the Soviet breakup, tourist dollars would benefit nuclear safety by providing for reactor maintenance on chartered icebreakers that would be plying Russia's Northern Sea Route the rest of the year. In the final analysis, I'm not anti-nuclear enough to avoid using nuclear power where it already exists. I wouldn't keep the lights turned off in France, for example. *(Nikon F4, 16mm f2.8 lens, f4 at 2 seconds, Fuji Velvia)*

Open leads in the Arctic Ocean at the North Pole, Arctic Ocean; 1993 *p. 131*

When our icebreaker stopped at the North Pole, I was surprised to see open leads of water. While we were celebrating out on the ice, the sun came through the clouds for the first time in almost a week. I rushed up

onto the deck to take this photograph of mist rising off the open water from a high vantage point on a secure tripod—a carefully composed sharp image that would be impossible to match on a ground expedition or a flight to the pole. I used a Singh-Ray two-stop graduated neutral-density filter to hold the dark sky and still have detail in the water. *(Nikon F4, 80–200mm f2.8 lens, f5.6 at 1/250 second, Fuji Velvia)*

Wally Herbert, first person to the North Pole by nonmotorized means; 1993 *p. 131*

On our return from the pole, we detoured to rescue a ship stuck in the ice while attempting the first circumnavigation of Greenland. One of the stranded *Kapitan Khlebnikov*'s lecturers was Wally Herbert, whom I photographed on the bridge with the *Yamal* breaking a path in the distance. Herbert's first uncontested, nonmotorized surface journey to the North Pole was just one half of his first trans-Arctic traverse by dog team. He left Barrow, Alaska, on February 21, 1968, and arrived at the pole on April 6, 1969—sixty years to the day after Peary claimed to have stood there. Analysis of Peary's incomplete diaries, measurements, and public statements strongly suggests that he in fact failed to reach the pole and was aware of his failure. His team members who were making independent latitude observations were asked to go back just before his final "dash to the pole," on which Peary reported major increases in miles traveled per day that have not been matched by modern expeditions. Peary's claim gained acceptance after Frederick Cook's even more vague one to have reached the pole a year earlier was rejected in the wake of a scandal over his having faked the first ascent of Mount McKinley (see page 103). Before then, a 1909 newspaper poll showed 96 percent of the public believing Cook; 24 percent, Peary. The National Geographic Society, a Peary sponsor, appointed a committee staffed with Peary supporters that publicly validated his "proofs," but then sequestered them for almost eighty years until doubt fanned by a CBS TV documentary prompted the magazine to have Wally Herbert check the data and write an honest assessment. Herbert's September 1988 *National Geographic* article concluded that Peary had no proof of reaching the pole and, given the benefit of many doubts, likely came no closer than 30 to 60 miles of it. Other polar experts suggest Peary was at least 100 miles away. The magazine then asked the Navigation Foundation of Maryland to reexamine the evidence, especially the photographs. After their January 1990 article staunchly supported Peary's success, *Scientific American* printed a rebuttal from a disgruntled photo analyst hired by the Navigation Foundation. The *Washington Post* reported that the foundation's claim that Amundsen took no longitude readings to reach the South Pole was untrue and that his original notes in an Oslo archive, unlike Peary's, clearly plot his ground track. A display at *National Geographic* headquarters now cautiously states: "Peary determined he had reached the pole" and "many have challenged Peary's claim." The bottom line is that if Peary is given credit for reaching the North Pole at a possible distance of over 100 miles, we should also credit Shackleton with reaching the South Pole in 1908 after an honest, documented declaration of turning back at 97 miles. *(Nikon F4, 35–70mm f2.8 lens, SB-25 flash, f5.6 at 1/125 second, Fuji Velvia)*

Solar parhelion over cosmic ray detectors at the Amundsen-Scott South Pole Station, Antarctica; 1992 *p. 132*

A scientist checks a phased array of sensors for the "South Pole Air Shower Experiment" installed in 1988 to use the earth's atmosphere as a detector for charged particles created by cosmic background radiation. When background radioactivity was first discovered around the turn of the century, it was attributed to an earth source. By 1910, measurements of stronger "cosmic rays" at higher altitudes farther from the

center of the earth suggested their origin in space, perhaps extremely long ago. The South Pole provides the earth's clearest window to the cosmos because of its 9,300-foot altitude, near absence of water vapor, unparalleled atmospheric clarity, low level of background radiation "noise," six months of darkness, and vantage point for continuous observation of the same sky poised directly over the earth's axis. My own informal study of outdoor optical effects, combined with published polar observations by Dr. Robert Greenler, led me to center a solar parhelion on the ladder just before the scientist ventured up. The rainbowlike circle with a 22° angular radius is caused by sunlight refracting from airborne ice crystals. *(Nikon f4, 20mm f4 lens, f16 at 1/125 second, Fuji Velvia)*

Self-portrait at the South Pole, Antarctica; 1992 *p. 132*

I made this self-portrait at the South Pole with a self-timer on an electronic Nikon equipped with a remote lithium battery wired into my warm pocket. For the previous half hour, I had been taking pictures in -45°F temperatures until I noticed that my LCD display was blank. I thought the battery was dead, yet the shutter still released. Having read that LCDs stop at temperatures below -30°F, I was reasonably sure that the camera's meter and shutter were still functioning—but not *that* sure. To shoot easily with gloves on, I had set the camera on automatic exposure with a +.7 exposure compensation for the bright snow. Before attempting more science photos, I decided to walk over to the pole and use up the rest of the roll. I put the camera on a tripod, hung the battery pack with it, and used the self-timer to finish the roll. Afterward, I reshot the self-portraits for "insurance" with a Nikon F4 powered by a special nicad pack. Both takes came out perfectly. Ever since, I've left my mechanical backup camera home on polar journeys. *(Nikon F4, 35–70mm f2.8 lens, f5.6 at 1/250 second, Fuji Velvia)*

Cathleen McDermott growing vegetables in a greenhouse at the Amundsen-Scott South Pole Station, Antarctica; 1992 *p. 132*

The Amundsen-Scott South Pole Station is isolated from the rest of the world for over eight months of the year. About twenty-five scientists and support staff spend the winter, between summers when more than 125 people involved with thirty science projects may be working at the station. In April 1992, a greenhouse was built to provide fresh vegetables for the workers. Here, Cathleen McDermott pollinates peppers and cucumbers in temperatures over 80°F above zero, while outside winter temperatures have dropped as low as -117°F. I used a Photoflex soft box to provide soft foreground light, but my major difficulty was trying to stop my lens from fogging after stepping from dry polar cold into a humid artificial tropical environment. *(Nikon F4, 24mm f2.8 lens, SB-25 flash, f5.6 at 1/8 second, Fuji Velvia)*

Dr. Stephen Warren collecting pure snow samples 70 feet above the South Pole, Antarctica; 1992 *p. 133*

Dr. Stephen Warren, a professor of geophysics and atmospheric sciences at the University of Washington, spent almost a year at the South Pole studying the optical and physical properties of the Antarctic snow surface. He was especially concerned with how the surface reflects thermal infrared radiation back into the atmosphere. He didn't trust snow samples taken on the ground, where they might have been

contaminated by motors and human activity at the pole, so he set up a collector on top of a 70-foot meteorological tower. His work has broad implications for interpreting satellite data and correlating amounts of trace chemicals in the atmosphere, such as sulfates that may arrive either naturally from volcanoes or artificially from pollution, with those deposited in the snow. He became so accustomed to the winter conditions that he described a 25-knot wind in -40°F air as "a brisk, warm wind."

Warren, the most senior scientist ever to winter over at the South Pole, also became a member of the 300 Club: after fifteen minutes in a 200°F sauna, and with the outside temperature below -100°F, he ran to the pole, naked except for his running shoes. He later measured the temperature atop the "met tower" to be a balmy -88°F, because of an inversion, when it was an even -100°F 2 meters above the ground. *(Nikon F4, 16mm f2.8 lens, f8 at 1/125 second, Fuji Velvia)*

Dr. Jeffrey Peterson and Hien Nguyen doing cosmic ray studies at the South Pole, Antarctica; 1992 *p. 133*

In an astrophysics lab a mile from the South Pole, Dr. Jeffrey Peterson and Hien Nguyen are assembling an instrument for an experiment code-named COBRA—Cosmic Background Radiation Anisotropy. To induce extreme superconductivity for their detector, they need to cool a piece of metal well below the -40°F outside their door. The adiabatic demagnetization refrigeration device will bring it down to .05° Kelvin, a hair above absolute zero at -459.6°F.

Princeton University researchers have come to the South Pole since 1986 to definitively test current theories of the origin of the universe by studying cosmic microwave background radiation in the best possible environment. Most astrophysicists believe that the microwaves are greatly redshifted radiation from the glowing of the newborn exploding universe in the first

100,000 years after the Big Bang. At other astronomical sites, such as the top of Mauna Kea in Hawaii where the air is ten times more clouded by water vapor, the background radiation appears to be even, but because the universe is not spread evenly, the ancient radiation should also have traces of definable "lumpiness" that could help assemble a ghostly image of "the seeds of structure" of today's universe. The task involves asking and answering questions that, as Barry Lopez puts it, "are larger by far than the imagination, the vision of any one person." Earlier in 1992, a complex airborne experiment had strongly confirmed nonrandom form in cosmic background radiation.

When I wrote down the name of Peterson's assistant, Hien Nguyen, I asked him if he was Vietnamese. Yes. In 1982, he had arrived in America as a boat person who couldn't speak English. Ten years later he was a Princeton graduate student on the cutting edge of astrophysics. *(Nikon N90, 24mm f2.8 lens, SB-25 flash, f8 at 1/60 second, Fuji Velvia)*

Evening sun on a pressure ridge, Arctic Ocean, near Barrow, Alaska; 1994 *p. 134*
While standing for days with Eskimo whalers beside pressure ridges on the frozen Arctic Ocean, I became attuned to subtle color differences that have meaning for whaling, survival—and photography. A dark line in the gray sky means an open lead in the distance where whales might be found. A yellowish spot in the overall bluish cast of the ice might be a polar bear (one later appeared within sight of this pressure ridge). Vivid blues were what I was looking for to maximize the visual power of ice photographs. In Antarctica, a tourist can wait on the deck for just the right iceberg to go by in just the right light. Here, I began assembling a mental image of my ideal photograph from the static scene around me days before I finally took it. I wanted to juxtapose patterns of

rich blues with warmer tones. When I looked closely, the backlit spaces on the shady side of raised ice blocks were deep blue, but as I stood back, the surrounding brightness destroyed the impression. I chose a wall of blocks with a strong pattern that faced north and waited for a rare bit of low-angled direct sunlight. When one evening the sun finally broke beneath the clouds, I metered a five-stop difference between the bright sky and the blue shadows of my chosen wall. I stacked two Singh-Ray graduated neutral-density filters over my lens to balance the light intensities without altering color response. Without the filters, the scene was far outside the film's range. I could have rendered a sky with this tone against an almost black foreground, or deep blue ice against a washed-out sky, but not both together. *(Nikon N90, 85mm f2 lens, f16 at 1/2 second, Fuji Velvia)*

Eskimo girls riding bicycles in winter, Barrow, Alaska; 1994 *p. 134*
While driving an old truck through the residential streets of Barrow in winter, I spotted two Inupiat Eskimo girls coming out of their homes with their bicycles. I wanted to take closer pictures, but out of habit stayed back and, knowing the girls were unaware of the camera, first took this "insurance" shot with 600mm magnification braced on the roof of the truck. After I walked up and got their permission to take tighter shots, nothing worked as well as this candid scene where they are standing together about to take off. The light was so dim beneath heavy fog near the end of a short winter day that my closer shots of them riding were either too blurred by motion or filled with distracting glares off the snow when I tried to use fill-flash. *(Nikon N90, 300mm f2.8 lens with 2X teleconverter, f2.8 at 1/60 second, Kodak Lumiere 100)*

Winter in Barrow, Alaska; 1994 *p. 135*
On a cold winter evening, I walked through Barrow with my camera and tripod looking for a typical residential scene. I wanted to capture the feeling of a place where the sun sets in November and doesn't rise again until late January. I also wanted to show how the town's outward appearance gives no clue that it is the center of what may well be the world's richest municipality. Once a sleepy Eskimo village with no city services, Barrow entered the twentieth century in the sixties, passed through it in the seventies and eighties, and now exists within a world of its own that has state-of-the-art social services exceeding those of every major American city on a per capita basis. Barrow's 3,500 residents make up over half the population of the North Slope Borough, which is even larger than it is wealthy. No other municipal government comes close to the land area of this Minnesota-sized "city" that was incorporated in 1972. It includes virtually every Eskimo living north of the crest of the Brooks Range who would benefit from the 1971 Native Claims Settlement Act, which ordered the largest redistribution of federal lands of the century. The borough receives over $100 million a year in property taxes on the Prudhoe Bay oilfield and is Alaska's largest employer. Seventy percent of its residents are native. Other income comes from native corporations with thousands of shareholders, which now have major land and resource holdings as well as hotels, construction companies, and engineering firms. But Barrow also has an extremely high cost of living and many families living at poverty level. I bought a gallon of milk for $6.59 and visited a tiny, unfurnished apartment that rents for $1,500 per month. After Barrow citizens voted to ban the sale or possession of alcohol on November 1, 1994, crime dropped radically, but by early 1995 petitions to revoke the ban were being circulated. Many residents expect the ban to clean up the town's image in a more literal

way by reducing the great amount of casual litter that surfaces each spring when the snow melts. *(Nikon F4, 35mm f1.4 lens, f2 at 1/2 second, Kodak Lumiere 100)*

Indoor playground, Ipalook Elementary School, Barrow, Alaska; 1994 *p. 135*
The North Slope Borough spends over $20,000 per student per year for education and related community facilities, such as this giant, heated indoor playground within a $62.5 million elementary school—the most expensive in the nation. As I set up my obviously expensive Nikon with flash on the floor of the school's indoor playground, an Inupiat boy of seven asked me my name and where I was from. When I said California, he glanced at my camera bag, looked me in the eye, and, after a long silence, asked, "When you go away, do you lock your doors so the robbers don't get you?" He said he didn't want to visit California, because he'd seen what it was like on television. *(Nikon F4, 20mm f2.8 lens, f2.8 at 1/4 second, Kodak Lumiere 100)*

Eskimo basketball in winter, Barrow, Alaska; 1994 *p. 135*
On a -28°F winter day, I photographed two Inupiat Eskimo teenagers playing basketball in their front yard, unfazed by the wind chill of a stiff breeze coming off the sea ice. They thought there was nothing unusual about what they were doing and asked why I was taking pictures of basketball. Watching them made me decide to

go running for the first time since I had arrived in Barrow, several days before. After the first mile, I had to strip off my pile jacket because I was overheated. I kept running for forty minutes, staying toasty in just polypropylene long underwear with a thin wind shell. When I stopped for a minute to talk to a man feeding his dogs, I began to shiver. *(Nikon N90, 80–200mm f2.8 lens, f4 at 1/500 second, Fuji Velvia)*

Mountain of compacted trash, McMurdo Station, Ross Island, Antarctica; 1992 *p. 136*
On morning runs between the U.S. McMurdo Station and New Zealand's Scott Base, I noticed a growing mountain of cubed cans stacked in an open lot, waiting to be picked up by a ship that arrives once a year. One clear day I took along a camera, flash unit, and small tripod to make this shot. I then ditched my equipment in the rocks, completed my run, and picked up my gear on the way back. The cans were part of a new recycling program at McMurdo. In earlier decades trash had been tossed in an open landfill or bulldozed into the nearby bay, which is now seriously polluted with hydrocarbons and PCBs. The National Science Foundation says that plans for a McMurdo cleanup were well under way before a highly publicized Greenpeace campaign set up a base at nearby Cape Evans in Antarctica in 1987. A live protest was staged at McMurdo with signs reading "Clean it up or shut it down." Many observers doubt Congress would have authorized $30 million in 1989 for a five-year cleanup plan were it not for the adverse publicity. These cans were shipped out with 2,851 tons of waste, including trash removed from the old landfill along with several feet of contaminated ground beneath it. *(Nikon N90, 28–70mm f3.5 lens, f5.6 at 1/250 second, Fuji Velvia)*

Ice cave in Erebus Glacier Tongue, McMurdo Sound, Ross Island, Antarctica; 1992 *p. 136*
I was invited to explore this newly found cave with guides from McMurdo Station to see if it was safe enough to use for recreational visits by scientists and employees on weekends. It looks something like a movie set because it has a level floor that preexisted the formation of the cave. The glacial ice of the Erebus Glacier Tongue is slowly creeping out over the sea ice of McMurdo Sound, driven by the pressure of ice high on 12,447-foot Mount Erebus. Every few decades, a giant section of the tongue several miles long breaks off and floats away. Meanwhile, a visitor can experience large cracks in the glacial ice, not as crevasses from above, but as caves from below that can be walked through on a level floor of sea ice. As I watched the guides explore a side room, their headlamps cast a warm glow that set it apart from the deep blue walls of the crevasse. To recreate that visual impression without the harsh streaking of lights of a normal time exposure, I asked one of my companions to set off my flash unit in the side room during a four-second exposure. *(Nikon F4, 24mm f2.8 lens, SB-25 flash, f5.6 at 4 seconds, Fuji Velvia)*

Moonrise over Mount Erebus and McMurdo Station, Ross Island, Antarctica; 1992 *p. 137*

On my first evening in McMurdo in the early October spring, the moon rose above Mount Erebus into an absolutely clear sky above pink alpenglow on the peak. I attempted to make pristine photos over pressure ridges near the edge of the Ross Sea, but failed to produce anything I liked owing to the ubiquitous presence of human intrusions. I later found several places where I could have made images with a wholly wild character, but I had had no chance to scout the area first. I made this photograph after the sun went down on that first evening, during a drive out toward the runway on the sea ice with Guy Guthridge of the NSF. The twinkling lights of McMurdo beneath the moon and the volcano made the base appear like a fairy-tale village. I used a long exposure with a telephoto lens on a tripod to capture that impression. *(Nikon F4, 80–200mm f2.8 lens, f2.8 at 8 seconds, Fuji Velvia)*

Rooftop view of McMurdo Station, Ross Island, Antarctica; 1992 *p. 137*
Viewed up close, McMurdo Station looks like one of those typical industrial suburbs that encrust the perimeters of large American cities beyond the control of strict planning and zoning. Tourists on the first cruise that visited McMurdo in 1968 returned home to make scathing reports to Congress and the State Department. On my first day in Mac Town, senior National Science Foundation representative David Bresnahan took me on a drive to a high overlook, where the base assumed more of a semblance of order. Noting that my expression of awe was not entirely joyful, he said that if McMurdo looked ugly now, I should have seen it a few years earlier. The pleasantly level place where I was standing was once the site of a nuclear reactor that had been removed in 1972 because it wasn't efficient enough. Later,

about 40,000 cubic feet of contaminated rock were removed for environmental reasons. The infamous open dump had been cleaned up earlier in 1992. The gleaming metal roof of the largest building drew my eye to the brand-new $25 million Crary Lab, which was replacing a hodgepodge of outmoded buildings that were in the process of being torn down. Although McMurdo is indeed changing, this photograph closely parallels the memories of my first impressions. *(Nikon F4, 35–70mm f2.8 lens, f5.6 at 1/125 second, Fuji Velvia)*

National Science Foundation meeting, McMurdo Station, Ross Island, Antarctica; 1992 *p. 137*
Building 167, better known as "the Chalet," is the administrative headquarters at McMurdo Station for both the National Science Foundation and their private contractor, Antarctic Support Associates. In contrast to the assortment of portable military quonsets, metal sheds, wooden-box dorms with tiny windows, and weathered lab buildings dating back to the fifties, the stylish A-frame of the Chalet with its open cathedral ceiling looks more like a celebrity's Aspen winter home. From a balcony above the central conference room, I used an ultra-wide 15mm lens on a tripod to capture an air safety meeting in progress. The urban appearance inside the chalet can be deceptive. One step outside is wild Antarctica. During a discussion with senior NSF representative David Bresnahan in his office, a report came over the radio of an accident out on the ice. Bresnahan was out the door and in his truck in seconds, toting everything he needed in a survival bag that all personnel are required to have at the ready. His instant participation effected the rapid evacuation of a seriously injured man. *(Nikon F4, 15mm f3.5 lens, f5.6 at 1/2 second, Fuji Velvia)*

Acknowledgments

I am indebted to Dr. Luis Proenza for planting the seed that grew into this book. As Vice Chancellor for Research at the University of Alaska in 1988, he urged that I do a book on polar research supported by the United States government. I thought such a project sounded too lengthy and costly, but soon embarked on the broader one that took seven years to become this book.

Barbara and I applied for a 1989 NSF Antarctic Artists and Writers Program grant to do field research for a visual book that would blend polar natural history and cultural history with essential landscapes of ice, earth, air, and water. Guy Guthridge, manager of the NSF Polar Information Program, shepherded our vague proposal for nearly four years until we were approved for late 1992. At the last minute, Barbara had to stay back because of mouth injuries from an earlier rafting accident.

Meanwhile, Barbara and I had led a shorter InnerAsia Expeditions Antarctic photo tour aboard a Russian icebreaker chartered by Quark Expeditions. In 1993, Barbara and I lectured on other Quark icebreakers bound for the North Pole and the Weddell Sea. We wish to thank all who offered support or insights on our Antarctic journeys, including Robin Abbott, Dale Andersen, Don Barch, Beez Bohner, Peter Braddock, Dave Bresnahan, Rick Campbell, Michael Castellini, Neelon Crawford, Tim Cully, Nelia Dunbar, Toby Everett, Sam Feola, Erica Frost, Mimi Fujino, Guy Guthridge, Richard Hirsch, Markus Horning, Bryan Johnson, Jeff Keho, Charles Knight, Carsten Kooyman, Jerry Kooyman, Tory Kooyman, Kristin Larson, Steve Lewis, John Lynch, Cathleen McDermott, Mike McDowell, Bill McIntosh, Dave Marchant, Mike Messick, Colin Monteath, Greg Mortimer, Henry Perk, Jeff Peterson, Paul Ponganis, Al Read, David Rootes, Dave Rosenthal, Rod Rozier, Jim Sano, John Splettstoesser, Carol Stoker, Bernard Stonehouse, Ward Testa, Sean Turner, Scott Tyler, Harry Van Loon, Jill Vereyken, Ting Wang, Steve Warren, Bob Wharton, Ian Whillans, Red Whittaker, Peter Wilkniss, Terry Wilson, and Warren Zapol.

In the Arctic, where science and tourism are not as centralized, we horse-traded a photo workshop to bush pilot Vern Kingsford for air time and photos yet to be made to John Hobbie for a visit to Toolik Field Station. After frequent-flier miles took me to Barrow in winter, Marie Adams and Geoff Carroll extended gracious hospitality and shared their extensive knowledge of the Arctic. The Eskimo Whaling Commission permitted me to join the crew of whaling captain Thomas Brower III, who went to great effort to make both my coverage and his hunt highly successful. Biologist Jim Halfpenny invited Barbara and me to photograph polar bears with him in Churchill. Warren LaFave of Kluane Airways of Whitehorse and John Witham of Ross River flew me around the splendid subarctic Yukon and into the remote Cirque of the Unclimbables in the Northwest Territories.

I am deeply indebted to the publications and editors who gave me Arctic assignments that resulted in images for this book. David Friend of *Life* sent me to Greenland via Iceland (a subarctic island not included owing to space limitations). Harriet Choice of Universal Press Syndicate sent me to run dogs in the Brooks Range in winter. Joan Tapper of *Islands* assigned me to photograph in the Russian Arctic. Much earlier, Bob Gilka of *National Geographic* gave me two assignments on Mount McKinley.

We also wish to thank all who offered support or insights on our journeys to the Far North, including Billy Adams, Stephen Atkinson, Alan Bard, Brandon Benson, Oliver Brower, Patrick Brower, Price Brower, Robert Brower, Loren Buck, Art Davidson, Mark Dornblaser, Dan Endres, Craig George, Ned Gillette, Mikhail Grosswald, Chad Gubaly, Wally Herbert, Clive Holland, Larry Irish, Johnny Johnson, Jerry Jordan, Jim McCarthy, Bill Mackey, Jennelle Marcereau, Holmes Miller, Steve Miller, Greg Mortimer, Pelle Norit, Susan Patkotak, Doug Peacock, Susan Polischuk, Barbara Rexford, Nora Rexford, NorDell Rexford, Qinygan Rexford, Dennis Schmitt, Darrel Schoeling, Doug Seus, Michael Sewell, Lewis Shapiro, Arnold Small, Misha Stishov, Bradley Thompson, Lars Ulsoe, Sergey Vartanyan, Anna Vdovenko, Doug Weins, Margaret Werner, Barbara Williams, and Chuck Williams.

I must also mention my debt to others who helped shape my vision on twenty earlier journeys into Arctic and subarctic Alaska, Canada, Norway, and Siberia since 1972 that did not make it into this book (including Barbara's 1986 flight north of the Arctic Circle in our Cessna, when all our aerial photographs were ruined by a film defect). ARCO assisted my photography at Prudhoe Bay, as did Exxon USA in Prince William Sound after the oil spill.

All photographs in this book were made with Nikon 35mm cameras. I wish to thank Nikon Inc. for technical support as well as direct support toward the quality publication of this book. Much of my success with cold-weather photography is also due to use of fine specialty products. Marmot down clothing kept me warm in wind chill exceeding -100°F. Grabber hand and toe warmers enabled me to shoot photos on runs and fast scrambles in subzero conditions wearing Helly-Hansen mitts and New Balance running shoes. Electronic Nikons kept on clicking with Energizer AA lithium batteries and accessories from Kirk Enterprises, Photoflex, Really Right Stuff, and Singh-Ray.

We wish to thank James Clark, director of the University of California Press, for a fine relationship on a book packaged by our own Mountain Light Press. I acted as editorial director with lots of valuable input from Barbara, while Anne Canright, David Sweet, and Barbara Youngblood handled text editing, and Kristen Wurz did computer layout and composition following Steve Renick's design. Marcia Mason managed text corrections. Chris Bettencourt, Gary Crabbe, and Inger Hogstrom worked with transparencies and scanned images. After we were finished, Tony Crouch of UC Press oversaw the book's production.

Quotations by Barry Lopez from his 1986 book *Arctic Dreams* and from articles that appeared in *Harper's* magazine are reprinted with his kind permission. Manuscript readers who provided valuable comments include: Marie Adams, Suzie Eastman, Stephanie Fay, Craig George, Guy Guthridge, James Halfpenny, Richard Hirsch, John Hobbie, Jerry Kooyman, Colin Monteath, Paulann Thurmon, Bob Wharton, and Warren Zapol.

Photographs on pages 39, 111, 121, and 126 are by Barbara Cushman Rowell; those on pages 91 and 125 are by Bill Mackey and Jules Uberuaga with my camera. No photographs in this book are digitally altered beyond normal prepress except for the background images behind the title spread on pages 2 and 3 that have been bled more evenly to white to fit the design. All photographs of captive or controlled animals are clearly disclosed. Lens and exposure information was not originally recorded and has been recalled as best as possible. Exhibit prints, traveling shows, or stock use of any image in this book may be arranged through Mountain Light Photography of Emeryville, California (510-601-9000).

Index

180

POLES APART

*was created and produced at Mountain Light Press
in Emeryville, California, in association with
the University of California Press.*

*Written and produced by Galen Rowell
Edited by Anne Canright, David Sweet, and Barbara Youngblood
Computer-generated layout by Kristen Wurz
Transcription by Marcia Mason
Designed by Steve Renick*

*Layout and composition on an Apple
Macintosh using Aldus PageMaker software,
Adobe Garamond and Centaur typefaces, and
images digitized for position on a Barneyscan.*

*Color separations stochastically screened with
a random dot and proofed initially in digital form on the Iris system,
printing on 150gsm Veitsiluoto Matte paper. Printed and
bound in Hong Kong through Mandarin Offset.*

ARCTIC

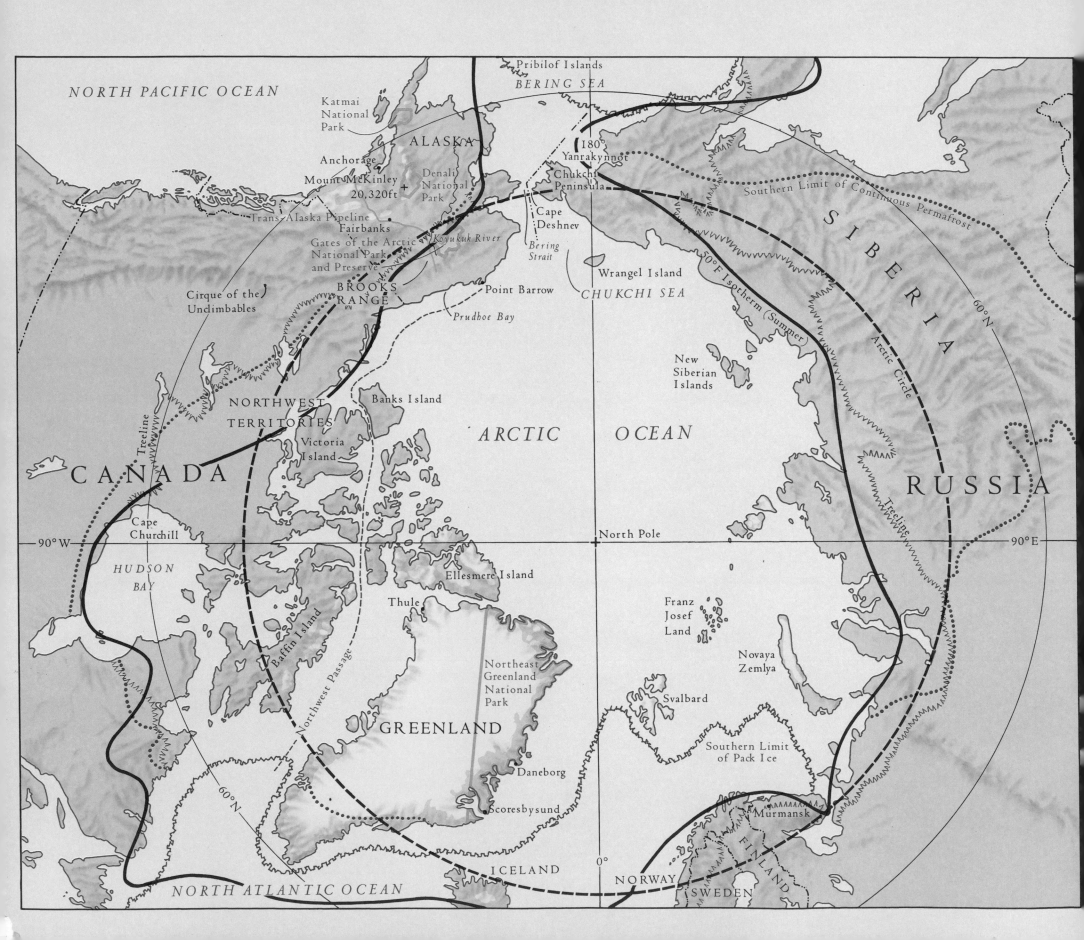

NORTH PACIFIC OCEAN

Pribilof Islands
BERING SEA

Katmai National Park

ALASKA

180°
Yanrakynnot
Chukchi Peninsula

Anchorage
Mount McKinley 20,320ft

Denali National Park

Cape Deshnev

Southern Limit of Continuous Permafrost

SIBERIA

60°N

Trans-Alaska Pipeline
Fairbanks
Gates of the Arctic National Park and Preserve

Koyukuk River

Bering Strait

Wrangel Island
CHUKCHI SEA

Cirque of the Unclimbables

BROOKS RANGE

Point Barrow

Prudhoe Bay

10°F Isotherm (Summer)

Arctic Circle

New Siberian Islands

NORTHWEST TERRITORIES

Banks Island

ARCTIC   OCEAN

RUSSIA

Treeline

CANADA

Victoria Island

Treeline

90°W

Cape Churchill

North Pole

90°E

HUDSON BAY

Ellesmere Island

Thule

Franz Josef Land

Baffin Island

Northwest Passage

Northeast Greenland National Park

Novaya Zemlya

Svalbard

GREENLAND

Southern Limit of Pack Ice

Daneborg

60°N

Scoresbysund

Murmansk

0°

ICELAND

NORWAY

FINLAND

NORTH ATLANTIC OCEAN

SWEDEN